W9-CNG-119

General Studies Series

TIMBER CONSTRUCTION FOR DEVELOPING COUNTRIES

Strength Characteristics and Design

UNIDO

UNITED NATIONS INDUSTRIAL DEVELOPMENT ORGANIZATION
Vienna, 1995

Material in this publication may be freely quoted or reprinted, but acknowledgement is requested, together with a copy of the publication containing the quotation or reprint.

The views expressed are those of the individual authors and do not necessarily reflect the view of UNIDO.

TH
1101
.T557
1995

ID/SER.O/9

UNIDO PUBLICATION
UNIDO.92.9.E
ISBN 92-1-106297-7

SEP 02 1995

Explanatory notes

AITC	American Institute of Timber Construction
AS	Australian Standard
CSIRO	Commonwealth Scientific and Industrial Research Organization
TEW	Timber Engineering Workshop
UNIDO	United Nations Industrial Development Organization

PREFACE

Whether grown in a particular country or not, wood is a virtually universal material that is familiar to people all over the world. It is used for many purposes but principally for construction, furniture, packaging and other specialized uses such as transmission poles, railway ties, matches and household articles. The United Nations Industrial Development Organization (UNIDO), which was established in 1967 to assist developing countries in their efforts to industrialize, has the responsibility within the United Nations system for assisting in the development of secondary woodworking industries and has carried out this responsibility since its inception at the national, regional and interregional levels by means of projects both large and small. UNIDO also assists by preparing manuals on topics that are common to the woodworking sectors of most countries.*

The lectures presented at the Timber Engineering Workshop (TEW), held from 2 to 20 May 1983 at Melbourne, Australia, are part of the continuing efforts of UNIDO to help engineers and specifiers appreciate the role that wood can play as a structural material. Collected in the form of 38 chapters, these lectures have been entitled Timber Construction for Developing Countries, which forms part of the General Studies Series. Eight of the chapters make up this fourth volume of the collection, Strength Characteristics and Design. The TEW was organized by UNIDO with the cooperation of the Commonwealth Scientific and Industrial Research Organization (CSIRO) and was funded by a contribution made under the Australian Government's vote of aid to the United Nations Industrial Development Fund. Administrative support was provided by the Department of Industry and Commerce of the Australian Government. The remaining lectures (chapters), which cover a wide range of subjects, including case studies, are contained in four additional volumes, as shown in the table of contents.

Following the pattern established for other specialized technical training courses in this sector, notably the course on furniture and joinery and that on criteria for the selection of woodworking machinery,** the lectures were complemented by visits to sites and factories, discussion sessions and work assignments carried out by small groups of participants.

It is hoped that the publication of these lectures will lead to the greater use of timber as a structural material to help satisfy the tremendous need in the developing countries for domestic, agricultural, industrial and commercial buildings and for structures such as bridges. It is also hoped that the lectures will be of use to teachers in training institutes as well as to engineers and architects in public and private practice.

Readers should note that the examples cited often reflect Australian conditions and thus may not be wholly applicable to developing countries,

---

*These activities are described more fully in the booklet UNIDO for Industrialization: Wood Processing and Wood Products (PI/78).

**The lectures for these two courses were collected and published as Furniture and Joinery Industries for Developing Countries (United Nations publication, Sales No. E.88.III.E.7) and Technical Criteria for the Selection of Woodworking Machines (UNIDO publication, Sales No. 92.1.E).

despite the widespread use of the Australian timber stress grading and strength grouping systems and despite the wide range of conditions encountered on the Australian subcontinent. Moreover, it must be remembered that some of the technology that is mentioned as having been new at the time of the Workshop (1983) may since then have been further developed. Similarly, standards and grading systems that were just being developed or introduced at that time have now become accepted. Readers should also note that the lectures were usually complemented by slides and other visual aids and by informal comments by the lecturer, which gave added depth of coverage.

CONTENTS*

*For the reader's convenience the contents of the four complementary vol-
umes are also given here.

Figures

Introduction to Wood and Timber Engineering
(ID/SER.0/6)

   I. Forest products resources
      W. E. Hillis

  II. Timber engineering and its applications in developing countries
      John G. Stokes

 III. Wood, the material
      W. E. Hillis

  IV. Mechanical properties of wood
      Leslie D. Armstrong

   V. Conversion of timber
      Mervyn W. Page

  VI. Seasoning of structural timber
      F. J. Christensen

Structural Timber and Related Products
(ID/SER.0/7)

    I. Characteristics of structural timber
       Robert H. Leicester

   II. Structural grading of timber
       William G. Keating

  III. Proof grading of timber
       Robert H. Leicester

   IV. Model of the timber grading process
       Robert H. Leicester

    V. Visual grading of timber
       J. Hay

   VI. Review of timber strength systems
       William G. Keating

  VII. The properties and end uses of a range of wood-based panel
       products
       Kevin J. Lyngcoln

 VIII. Structural plywood
       Lam Pham and Robert H. Leicester

   IX. Glued laminated timber
       Robert H. Leicester

    X. Adhesives for timber
       R. E. Palmer

Durability and Fire Resistance
(ID/SER.0/8)

I. Durability of timber
    John Beesley

II. Fire resistance of timber
    Robert H. Leicester

Applications and Examples
(ID/SER.0/10)

I. Specification of timber for structural use
    William G. Keating

II. Plywood in concrete formwork
    Kevin J. Lyngcoln

III. Timber structures: detailing for durability
    Leslie D. Armstrong

IV. Use of green timber in structures
    Leslie D. Armstrong

V. Pole structures
    G. B. Walford

VI. Timber framing for housing
    Bernie T. Hawkins

VII. Case study of timber construction: Kenya hotel
    Peter A. Campbell

VIII. Case study of timber construction: New Zealand
    G. B. Walford

IX. Case study of timber construction: South-East Asia
    John R. Tadich

X. Stress grades and timber construction economies, exemplified by
    the UNIDO prefabricated timber bridge
    C. R. Francis

XI. Efficient timber structures using metal connectors
    E. E. Dagley

XII. Construction experiences in developing countries
    C. R. Francis

INTRODUCTION

Many developing countries are fortunate in having good resources of timber, but virtually all countries make considerable use of wood and wood products, whether home-grown or imported, for housing and other buildings, in both structural and non-structural applications, as well as for furniture and cabinet work and specialized uses. Although wood is a familiar material, it is all too often misunderstood or not fully appreciated since it exists in a great variety of types and qualities.

Some species, such as teak, oak and pine, are well known almost everywhere while others, such as beech, eucalyptus, acacia, mahogany and rosewood, are known primarily in particular regions. Still others, notably the merantis, lauans and keruing, which come from South-East Asia, have only recently been introduced to widespread use. Very many more species exist and are known locally and usually used to good purpose by those in the business. Also, plantations are now providing an increasing volume of wood.

The use of timber for construction is not new and, in fact, has a very long tradition. In many countries this tradition has unfortunately given way to the use of other materials - notably, concrete, steel and brick - whose large industries have successfully supported the development of design information and the teaching of methods for engineering them. This has not been so much the case for timber, despite considerable efforts by some research and development institutions in countries where timber and timber-framed construction have maintained a strong position. Usually the building methods are based on only a few well-known coniferous (softwood) species and a limited number of standard sizes and grades. For these, ample design aids exist, and relatively few problems are encountered by the very many builders involved.

Recent developments in computer-aided design and in factory-made components and fully prefabricated houses have led to better quality control and a decreased risk of site problems. Other modern timber engineering developments have enabled timber to be used with increasing confidence for an ever wider range of structures. This has been especially so in North America, Western Europe, Australia and New Zealand.

UNIDO feels that an important means of transferring this technology is the organization of specialized training courses that introduce engineers, architects and specifiers to the subject and draw their attention to the advantages of wood, as well as its disadvantages and potential problem areas, and also to reference sources. In this way, for particular projects or structures, wood will be fairly considered in competition with other materials and used when appropriate. Comparative costs, aesthetic considerations and tradition must naturally be taken into account in the context of each country and project, but it is hoped that the publication of these lectures will lead those involved to a rational approach to the use of wood in construction and remove some of the misunderstandings and misapprehensions all too often associated with this ancient yet modern material.

I. THE FRACTURE STRENGTH OF WOOD

Robert H. Leicester*

Introduction

Many types of structural timber elements can fail owing to fracture. This type of failure can be catastrophic because it occurs quickly in a brittle mode. Fracture can occur at any sharp discontinuity in a structure. These discontinuities are usually difficult to analyse and predictions of fracture strength must be based on prototype testing. However, there are many cases of practical interest in which the source of the potential fracture is the stress concentration at the root of a sharp notch located in an element subjected to a state of plane stress. Some examples of this are shown in figures 1 and 2. For such cases, the load to cause failure can be predicted quite accurately through the application of elastic fracture mechanics.

Figure 1. Examples of cracks

A. Butt joint in glulam

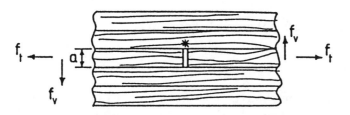

B. Crack in curved arch

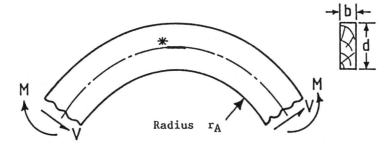

C. Longitudinal split in beam

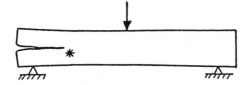

*Location of potential fracture

---

*An officer of CSIRO, Division of Building Research, Melbourne.

Figure 2. Examples of 90° notches

A. Glued lap joint

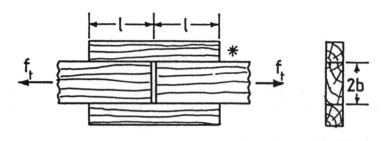

B. Notched beam

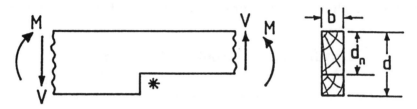

*Location of potential fracture

In the following, the basic concepts of elastic fracture mechanics and their application to the type of structural elements shown in figures 1 and 2 will be outlined briefly.

The following notation is used in this chapter:

a	= Crack length
b, b_o	= Member width
d, d_n	= Member depth
d_{cr}	= Dimension for critical size
F_v	= Average shear strength measured on small clear specimens
f_b, f_t, f_v	= Applied nominal stress in bending, tension and shear
$g(\theta)$, $h(\theta)$	= Functions of θ
K_A, K_B, K_I, K_{II}	= Stress intensity factors
K_{AC}, K_{BC}, K_{IC}, K_{IIC}	= Critical stress intensity factors
LR, RL, LT, TL, RT, TR	= Notation for crack orientation (see figure 7)

M   = Bending moment

r   = Distance from origin, a polar coordinate

r_A = Radius of arch

s, q   = Intensity constants

V   = Shear force

σ = Stress

σ_x, σ_y, σ_{xy} = Stress referenced to cartesian coordinates

x, y, z   = Cartesian coordinates

ρ = Density

A. Elastic fracture mechanics

1. Stress fields around notches

It can be shown [1] that for an element in a state of plane stress such as that shown in figure 3, the stress field in the vicinity of a notch root has the following form:

$$\sigma_x = g_1(\theta)K_A/(2\pi r)^s + h_1(\theta)K_B/(2\pi r)^q \qquad (1a)$$

$$\sigma_y = g_2(\theta)K_A/(2\pi r)^s + h_2(\theta)K_B/(2\pi r)^q \qquad (1b)$$

$$\sigma_{xy} = g_3(\theta)K_A/(2\pi r)^s + h_3(\theta)K_B/(2\pi r)^q \qquad (1c)$$

where x, y and r, θ are cartesian and polar coordinates, respectively, relative to the notch root; σ_x, σ_y and σ_{xy} are stresses; $g(\theta)$ and $h(\theta)$ denote functions of θ, and K_A, K_B, s and q are constants with s $\leq$ q.

Figure 3. Notation for stresses and notch root

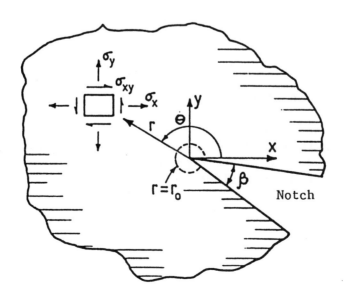

The terms $g(\theta)$, $h(\theta)$, K_A, K_B, s and q all depend on the elastic properties of the material and on the notch angle. In addition, K_A and K_B are proportional to the applied loads. For practical purposes, it is sufficiently accurate to use a single set of typical elastic properties for the fracture analysis of all species of timber.

2. Failure criteria

Figure 4 shows values of intensity constants s and q for four types of notches. The values s > 1 and q > 1 are of interest because equations (1) show that for these cases, a stress singularity exists at the notch root; i.e. as the distance r tends to zero, the stresses σ_x, σ_y and σ_{xy} tend to infinity.

The two stress fields associated with the intensity constants s and q are denoted the primary and secondary stress singularities, respectively. Except for the case of a sharp crack having notch angle $\beta = 0$, the condition s > q holds, and consequently the primary singularity dominates at the notch root.

Obviously equations (1) cannot hold true in the immediate vicinity of the notch root. However, if the non-linear effects occur only within some small circle $r = r_0$ located completely within the theoretical singular stress field, as shown in figure 3, then the stress conditions within the immediate vicinity of the notch root are determined only by the elastic stresses acting on the circle $r = r_0$. These stresses, in turn, are directly proportional to the stress intensity factor K_A, so the failure criteria may be stated as follows:

$$K_A = K_{AC} \qquad (2)$$

where K_{AC}, termed the critical stress intensity factor, is the theoretically computed value of K_A for the loading at which failure is noted to occur in laboratory tests.

For the special case when the notch is a sharp crack located along an axis of elasticity, s = q and both the primary and secondary singularities are of equal significance. Here the primary and secondary stress fields have symmetrical and antisymmetrical deformation modes, respectively. These are termed mode I and mode II deformations and are illustrated in figure 5. Correspondingly, the notations K_I and K_{II} are used for stress intensity factors in lieu of K_A and K_B. The associated critical stress intensity factors are denoted K_{Ic} and K_{IIc}. Thus the failure criterion for sharp cracks may be written

$$G(K_I/K_{Ic}, \ K_{II}/K_{IIc}) = 1 \qquad (3)$$

where G is some function of stress intensity factors.

Equations (2) and (3) indicate that to predict the fracture load on a structural element, it is necessary to compute the relevant stress intensity factor K_I, K_{II} or K_A for the type of loading to be used and to have available the results of experimental measurements of the relevant critical stress intensity factor K_{Ic}, K_{IIc} or K_A for the particular type of notch under consideration. These matters will be considered in the following sections.

Figure 4.   Examples of intensity constants

A.   Notation for notch type

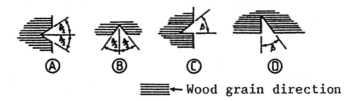

B.   Intensity constant s for primary stress field

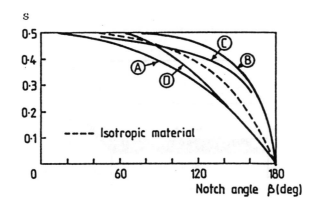

C.   Intensity constant q for secondary stress field

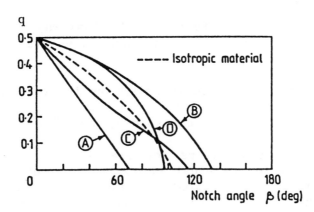

Figure 5. Displacement modes for cracks

A. Mode I

B. Mode II

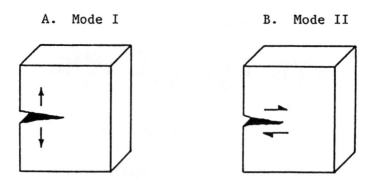

C. Mode III

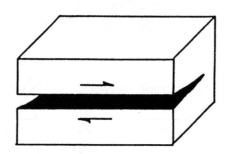

3. Size effect

A significant aspect of fracture strength that may not be readily apparent is that the form of the singularity functions in equations (1) implies a size effect on strength.

To derive the size effect, it is necessary to consider two geometrically similar structural elements subjected to the same type of loading. Reference to these two elements will be distinguished by use of the subscripts 1 and 2.

From dimensional considerations for elastic, geometrically similar elements, the ultimate applied external stress at fracture f_{u1} and the related internal stress $\sigma_1(r_1, \theta)$ on element 1, and the applied external stress at fracture f_{u2} and the related internal stress $\sigma_2(r_2, \theta)$ on element 2, are associated by

$$f_{u1}/\sigma_1(r_1, \theta) = f_{u2}/\sigma_2(r_2, \theta) \tag{4}$$

provided

$$r_1/d_1 = r_2/d_2 \tag{5}$$

where d_1 and d_2 denote the reference dimensions of the two members.

The notation $\sigma_1(r_1, \theta)$ is used to denote the value of the stress σ at the polar coordinate location r_1, θ in member 1.

From equations (1) and (2), the stresses near the notch root may be written

$$\sigma_1(r_1, \theta) = g(\theta)K_{AC}/(2\pi r_1)^s \tag{6}$$

$$\sigma_2(r_2, \theta) = g(\theta)K_{AC}/(2\pi r_2)^s \tag{7}$$

Equations (4) to (7) lead to

$$f_{u1}/f_{u2} = (d_2/d_1)^s \qquad (8)$$

Equation (8) shows that the nominal stress at fracture f_u is inversely proportional to d^s. Obviously, an upper bound to f_u is the strength of unnotched timber, denoted by F_u. The theoretical characteristic dimension d at which $f_u = F_u$ is termed the critical fracture length and is denoted by d_{cr}. The relationship between these parameters and the strength of real structural elements is illustrated in figure 6.

Figure 6. Illustration of effect of size on strength

A. Notation

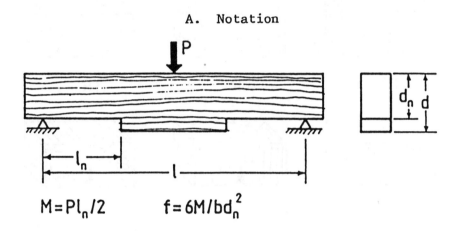

$$M = Pl_n/2 \qquad f = 6M/bd_n^2$$

B. Effect of size

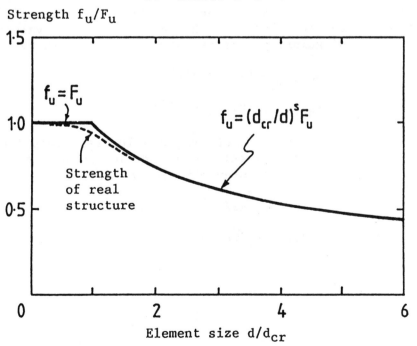

B. Fracture at sharp cracks

1. Stress intensity factors

Cracks are the special case of notches with zero notch angle. For the case of cracks lying along the principal axes of elasticity in wood, there are six possible types of orientation for cracks. These are illustrated in figure 7, in which the notations L, R and T refer to the longitudinal, radial and tangential directions, respectively. A two-letter notation is used to describe each crack; the first letter refers to the axis normal to the crack plane and the second refers to the direction in which the crack is pointing. Thus the six types of crack are denoted by LT, TL, LR, RL, TR and RT.

Figure 7. Notation for crack orientation

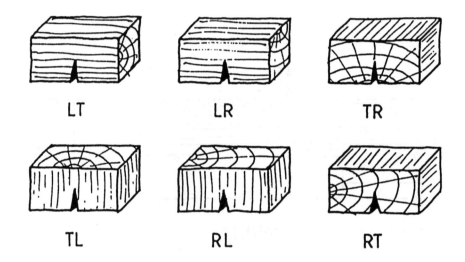

For all six types of cracks, the intensity constants s and q are equal to 0.5. In defining the stress intensity factors, the functions $g_2(\theta)$ and $h_3(\theta)$ in equations (1b) and (1c) are chosen so that at $\theta = \pi$ their values are $g_2(\theta) = h_3(\theta) = 1$. Hence the singularity stresses at $\theta = \pi$ are given by

$$\sigma_y\big|_{\theta=\pi} = K_I/(2\pi r)^{1/2} \tag{9}$$

$$\sigma_{xy}\big|_{\theta=\pi} = K_{II}/(2\pi r)^{1/2} \tag{10}$$

For the simplest case of a crack of length a located along the x-axis of elasticity of an infinite-sized element subjected to uniform stresses f_t and f_v as shown in figure 8, the stress intensity factors are

$$K_I = f_t(\pi a/2)^{1/2} \tag{11}$$

$$K_{II} = f_v(\pi a/2)^{1/2} \tag{12}$$

Figure 8. Notation for sharp crack

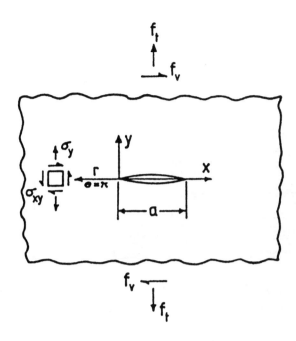

Stress intensity factors for many practical situations have been computed by Walsh [2, 3]. One example, shown in figure 9, relates to the effect of spacing of cracks such as occurs with butt joints in glulam beams. For this case, the mode I stress intensity factors are as follows [3]:

$$K_I = f_t \left\{ (\pi a/2)[4 + (s/a)]/[2 + (s/a)] \right\}^{1/2} \tag{13}$$

where a denotes the lamination width and s is the longitudinal spacing of the joints.

Figure 9. Spaced butt joints in adjacent laminations

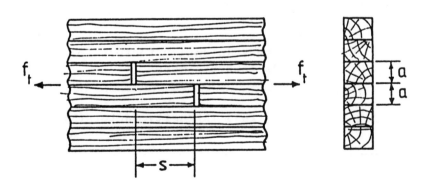

Barrett and Foschi [4] have derived K_{II}, the mode II stress intensity factors, for the case of end splits in beams such as that shown in figure 1A.

Stress intensity factors for timber elements that have not been formally analysed may be estimated by extrapolating the values computed for isotropic materials, such as those collated by Paris and Sih [5], or by the use of reasonable approximations. For example, from symmetry considerations it would be reasonable to assume that for a butt joint located in an edge lamination of width a, such as that shown in figure 10, the stress intensity factor must be roughly that of an internal butt joint in a lamination of width 2a. Hence the estimate for this case is

$$K_I \cong f_t [\pi a]^{1/2} \tag{14}$$

Figure 10. Edge butt joint

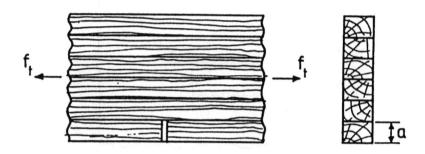

Similarly the stress intensity factors for the case of a crack in a curved arch subjected to a moment M and shear force V, as shown in figure 1B, may be estimated by equations (11) and (12), in which the values $f_t = 3M/2r_A bd$ and $f_v = 3V/2bd$ are used.

2. Critical stress intensity factors

The fracture strength for several types of sharp cracks in timber have been measured by Barrett [6], Leicester [7], Schniewind and Centeno [8], Walsh [9] and Wu [10]. From these data, an estimate of critical stress intensity factors based on density can be made, as shown in table 1. If it is required to relate critical stress intensity factors to the shear strength of clear timber, then the factors in table 1 may be transformed by the following relationship:

$$F_V = 0.018\rho \tag{15}$$

where F_V is the shear strength in MPa and ρ is the density in kg/m^3.

Table 1. Critical stress intensity factors for sawn cracks in dry timber

Crack orientation	Critical stress intensity factor (Nmm$^{-1.55}$)	
	K_{Ic}	K_{IIc}
LR, LT	0.15ρ	0.03ρ
RL, TL	0.02ρ	0.15ρ
RT, TR	0.02ρ	—

Note: ρ = density at 12 per cent moisture content, kg/m^3.

The values given in table 1 are a reasonable estimate for sawn cracks. For cracks formed by gluing, such as occur at butt joints in glulam, the critical stress intensity factors are on average about twice as great as those for sawn notches. However, because of the scatter of the data [7] it is recommended that for untested types of butt joints, the values shown in table 1 should also be used for glued cracks, with the added limitation that the maximum value used should not exceed the value given in table 1 for timbers with a density of 600 kg/m^3. Because of this poor correlation between fracture strength and density, it is recommended that for economical designs of butt-jointed laminae the rules be based on critical stress intensity factors that have been measured directly for each species/glue combination of interest.

The use of drill holes at notch roots to reduce stress concentration effects is common practice but does not appear to have a significant effect on fracture strength. In one set of measurements on cracks with LR and LT orientations [7], it was found that the effect of placing a drilled hole at the notch root was to increase K_{Ic} by a factor of only $(1 + 0.15\sqrt{r_h})$, where r_h is the radius of the hole expressed in millimetres.

3. Combined fracture modes

When both mode I and mode II stress fields are present, the failure criteria is found to be the following [7, 10]:

$$(K_I/K_{Ic}) + (K_{II}/K_{IIc})^2 = 1 \tag{16}$$

Equation (16) is illustrated in figure 11. It is valid throughout the range of both positive and negative stresses.

Figure 11. Failure criterion for combined modes

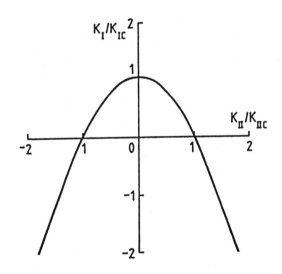

4. Example

The example will be to estimate the bending stress that will cause the fracture of a 20 mm thick bottom lamination of a glulam beam fabricated from a timber species having a density of 500 kg/m^3.

As noted earlier, a safe estimate of the fracture strength of notches formed through gluing can be obtained through use of the critical stress intensity factors for sawn cracks given in table 1. Thus, for a mode I failure of a crack with LT or LR orientation,

$$K_{Ic} = (0.15)(500) = 75 \ Nmm^{-1.5} \tag{17}$$

From equation (14) the applied stress intensity factor is

$$K_I = f_b[2 \times \pi \times 30]^{1/2} = 13.7 \ f_b \tag{18}$$

where f_b is the tension stress expressed in Nmm^{-2} occurring on the bottom lamination of the beam.

Hence for the failure criterion $K_I = K_{Ic}$, equations (17) and (18) lead to

$$f_b = 5.5 \ Nmm^{-2}$$

C. Fracture at right angle notches

1. Stress intensity factors

The right angle notch to be considered will be one with an edge located along the direction of the wood grain, as shown in figure 12. This direction will be denoted the x-axis. For this case, the intensity constant s has a value of 0.45 for typical timbers [1]. In defining the stress intensity factor, the function $g_2(\theta)$ in equation (1b) is chosen so that at the location $\theta = \pi$ as shown in figure 12, $g_2(\theta) = 1$ and the stress σ_y is then given by

$$\sigma_y/_{\theta = \pi} = K_A/(2\pi r)^{0.45} \tag{19}$$

Figure 12.   Notation for 90° notch

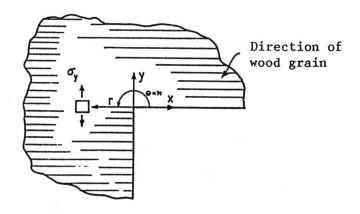

Walsh [3] has computed the stress intensity factors for several practical applications. For example, for the case of the glued lap joint shown in figure 2A, the stress intensity factor over the practical range of glued joints is roughly given by

$$K_A = f_t b^{0.45}[0.06 + 0.3(b/1)] \tag{20}$$

where the definitions of 1 and b are indicated in figure 2A.

Another example of practical significance is that of the notched beam shown in figure 2B. For beams with notch depths d_n/d in the range 0.3–0.7, the factors derived by Walsh [3], extended by examination of the test data obtained by Leicester and Poynter [11], lead to

$$K_A = d^{0.45}(0.05 \ f_b + 0.25 \ f_v) \tag{21}$$

where d is the maximum depth of the beam and $f_b = 6M/bd_n^2$ and $f_v = 3V/2bd_n$ are the nominal applied bending and shear stresses. For notch depths d_n/d outside the range 0.3–0.7, the stress intensity factor is reduced.

2. Critical stress intensity factors

For the case of sawn right angle notches in dry timber, the data by Leicester and Poynter [11] lead to the following:

$$K_{AC} = 0.015\,\rho \qquad\qquad (22)$$

where K_{AC} is the critical stress intensity factor in $Nmm^{-1.55}$ units and ρ is the density of timber in kg/m^3.

For the case of a glued lap joint such as that shown in figure 2A, the value of K_{AC} measured by Walsh, Leicester and Ryan [12] is about 20 per cent larger but shows more scatter.

3. Example

The problem is to estimate the load to cause fracture of the notched beam shown in figure 13. The density of the timber is 500 kg/m^3.

Figure 13. Example of a notched beam

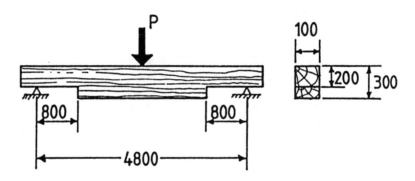

For a given load P, the nominal values of stress on the net cross-section are as follows:

$$f_b = (P/2)(800)(6/100 \times 200^2) = (6/10^4)P$$

$$f_v = (P/2)(1.5/100 \times 200) = (0.375/10^4)P$$

From equation (22),

$$K_{AC} = 500 \times 0.015 = 7.5 \ Nmm^{-1.55}$$

Finally, equation (21) and the failure criterion $K_A = K_{AC}$ lead to the following:

$$7.5 = (300)^{0.45}[(0.05)(6/10^4)P + (0.25)(0.375/10^4)P]$$

which gives P = 14,600 N, a force exerted by a load of 14,600/9.81 = 1,491 kg.

D. Concluding comment

In order to use the formal theory of elastic fracture mechanics to derive design recommendations, more information than is given herein is required. Examples of this additional information are the effects of duration of load, moisture content and natural defects such as knots and sloping grain. In addition, a knowledge of the variability in expected strength is required. Such information is not readily available in published form, although a limited set of data has been given by Leicester [7]. It is also to be noted that fracture mechanics predicts the onset of fracture at the notch root and does not necessarily indicate failure of a structural member. For example, the notched beam such as that shown in figure 13 may carry an increased load after fracture initiation if the timber is straight-grained.

Nevertheless, the use of fracture mechanics helps to ensure that the form of design recommendations is correct. An example would be the inclusion of the size effect discussed in section A.3. Several sections of AS 1720-1975 [13] are based on the formal application of elastic fracture mechanics.

Although this paper has been concerned with the fracture of elements in a state of plane stress, the research in fracture mechanics has covered other situations. For example, Westmann and Yang [14] have analysed cracked beams subjected to torsional forces and hence deformed in the mode III manner (figure 5).

Finally, it is of some interest to compare the fracture strength of timber with that of other materials. For the case of a 90° notch, the following are typical values:

Brickwork	$5 \text{ Nmm}^{-1.55}$
Plain concrete	$10 \text{ Nmm}^{-1.55}$
Timber	$10 \text{ Nmm}^{-1.55}$
Mild steel	$5,000 \text{ Nmm}^{-1.55}$

References

1. R. H. Leicester, "Some aspects of stress fields at sharp notches in orthotropic materials - I", Technological Paper No. 57 (South Melbourne, CSIRO, Division of Forest Products, 1971).

2. P. F. Walsh, "Linear fracture mechanics in orthotropic materials", Engineering Fracture Mechanics, vol. 4, 1972, pp. 533-541.

3. P. F. Walsh, "Linear fracture mechanics in orthotropic materials", Technical Paper (Second Series) No. 2 (Melbourne, CSIRO, Division of Building Research, 1974).

4. J. D. Barrett and R. O. Foschi, "Mode II stress-intensity factors for cracked wood beams", Engineering Fracture Mechanics, vol. 9, 1977, pp. 371-378.

5. P. C. Paris and G.C.M. Sih, "Stress analysis of cracks", ASTM Special Technical Publication No. 381, Symposium of Fracture Toughness Testing and its Applications (Chicago, 1964), pp. 30-81.

6. J. D. Barrett, "Fracture mechanics and the design of wood structures", <u>Royal Society of London: Philosophical Transactions</u>, Series A, vol. 299, 1981, pp. 217-226.

7. R. H. Leicester, "Fracture strength of wood", <u>Proceedings of First Australian Conference on Engineering Materials</u> (Sydney, University of New South Wales, 1974).

8. A. P. Schniewind and J. C. Centeno, "Fracture toughness and duration of load factor. I. Six principal systems of crack propagation, and the duration factor for cracks parallel to grain", <u>Engineering Fracture Mechanics</u>, vol. 2, 1971, pp. 223-233.

9. P. F. Walsh, "Cleavage fracture of timber", Technological Paper No. 65 (South Melbourne, CSIRO, Division of Forest Products, 1971).

10. E. M. Wu, "Application of fracture mechanics to anisotropic plates", <u>Journal of Applied Mechanics</u>, December 1967, pp. 967-974.

11. R. H. Leicester and W. G. Poynter, "On the design strength of notched beams", <u>Proceedings of 19th Forest Products Research Conference</u> (Melbourne, CSIRO, Division of Chemical and Wood Technology, 12-16 November 1979).

12. P. F. Walsh, R. H. Leicester and A. Ryan, "The strength of glued lap joints in timber", <u>Forest Products Journal</u>, vol. 23, No. 5 (May 1973), pp. 30-33.

13. Standards Association of Australia, <u>Australian Standard 1720-1975: SAA Timber Engineering Code</u> (Sydney, 1975).

14. R. A. Westman and W. H. Yang, "Stress analysis of cracked rectangular beams", <u>Journal of Applied Mechanics</u>, September 1967, pp. 693-701.

<u>Bibliography</u>

Leicester, R. H. Effect of size on the strength of structures. Technological paper No. 71. Melbourne. CSIRO, Division of Building Research, 1973.

Leicester, R. H. Applications of linear fracture mechanics in the design of timber structures. <u>In</u> Proceedings of 1974 Conference of the Australian fracture group. Melbourne, October 1974, pp. 156-164.

Leicester, R. H. <u>and</u> P. F. Walsh. Numerical analysis for notches of arbitrary notch angle. <u>In</u> Proceedings of 5th International Conference on fracture mechanics technology applied to material evaluation and structure design. Melbourne, August 1982.

II. TIMBER CONNECTORS

Edward P. Lhuede and Robert H. Leicester*

Introduction

The use of sawn and round timber in a range of structural applications is governed to a large extent by the availability of suitable fastening systems or components that permit the jointing of the members in a reliable and efficient manner. Over more than 50 years, design criteria for the common timber fasteners such as nails, screws, bolts, shear plates and split rings have evolved and have been consolidated by various workers; in somewhat more recent times, data on pressed steel nail plates and metal support brackets of various types have been added to the data on existing timber connectors and are listed in national timber design codes.

The data specified in such national codes will be relevant to the local conditions under which the particular fastener is to be used and may vary from country to country, but they will represent a reasonably reliable design figure.

The purpose of this lecture is first to provide an understanding of the behaviours of the various types of fasteners in use and then to establish bases from which design data relating to working loads and deflections or slip can be calculated for these connectors. As might be expected, the differing approaches of many investigators, particularly for transversely loaded nailed joints, have resulted in alternative procedures for specifying design data. It is not proposed to enter into a discussion of all the relevant information on any particular fastener, but the bases presented will have an overall or general acceptance and will be compatible, where relevant, within the range of data available.

A system of categorizing fasteners that has been adopted in both Australia (AS 1649) and the United States (ASTM D1761-77) lists fasteners under the following headings:

(a) Nails and screws under withdrawal and lateral loads;

(b) Bolts, and connectors requiring bolts for their use in three-member assemblies. Shear plates, split rings and dowel-type joints are included in this group;

(c) Nail plates and tooth plate connectors manufactured in a variety of thicknesses and with a range of tooth types;

(d) Light-gauge metal brackets used as joist hangers and brackets used as ties and frame supports.

Any grouping of fasteners into categories, such as the one used here, may be open to criticism, but it nevertheless forms a convenient basis for analysing performance.

---

*Officers of CSIRO, Division of Building Research, Melbourne.

The procedure will be to describe, where possible, a load-deflection curve for the connector and then establish a method for calculating the maximum load sustained by the joint. Particular aspects of the general use or behaviour will also be discussed.

A section on the cost of fasteners in timber construction is included.

A. Performance of nails and screws

1. Load-deflection curve for nail withdrawal

Figure 14 indicates a typical withdrawal load-deflection curve for a nail driven into the side grain of a medium-density hardwood. It shows that for a small displacement, the load is proportional to displacement and that once a limiting outward movement is exceeded, the joint fails. A measurable slip occurs at or near the peak load and a step-wise drop in load then accompanies increasing withdrawal distance.

Figure 14. Withdrawal load-displacement curve for a 3.16 mm diameter plain nail with 40 mm penetration in <u>E. regnans</u>, side grain

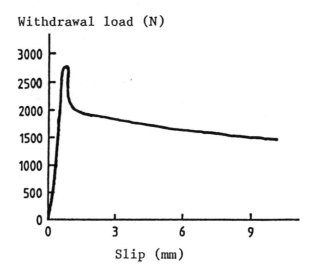

Figure 15 is a similar graph where the load has been taken up to a relatively low value, released, and then reapplied to a higher level. The chart has been stepped along the displacement axis to separate the subsequent reloadings, there having been ten separate loadings and unloadings before the maximum load was reached. Each load-deflection trace is approximately linear, although there is a degree of hysteresis in the unloading phase. This behaviour of the joint shows that the loading can be cycled up and down a linear region of the load-displacement curve.

Figure 16 shows the behaviour of a helically grooved, screw-type nail, which exhibits a load-displacement curve different from the curves of plain and annularly grooved nails. After an initial failure, the withdrawal load is seen to rise to a value greater than the first failure load at a significant displacement.

Figure 15. Load-displacement curves for a 3.16 mm diameter plain nail
with 40 mm penetration in <u>E. regnans</u>, side grain, repeated loading

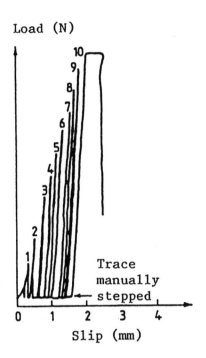

Figure 16. Load-displacement curve for 3.15 mm shank diameter, helically
grooved nail in <u>E. regnans</u>, side grain

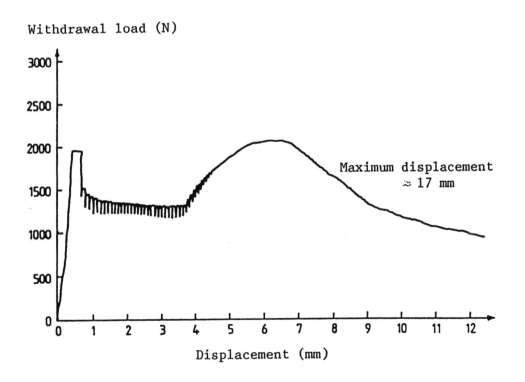

2. Maximum nail withdrawal loads

The work of Mack [1] covers a comprehensive range of timber densities ($350-1,200$ kg/m^3 on an air-dry basis at 12 per cent moisture content) and has established relationships between withdrawal resistance R, in N/mm of penetration, and density (table 2).

Table 2. Nail withdrawal resistance and density

Initial moisture content of timber	Time of test	Regression between withdrawal resistance R (N) and density D (kg/m^3) a/
Green	Immediate Three month delay before test	$R_{gi} = 24 \times 10^{-4}\, D_b{}^{1.4}d$ $R_{gd} = 0.14\, D_b{}^{0.7}d$
Dry	Immediate Three month delay before test	$R_{di} = 3.6 \times 10^{-5}\, D_b{}^{2.0}d$ $R_{dd} = 1.68 \times 10^{-4}\, D_d{}^{1.7}d$

a/ D_b is basic density, D_d is air-dry density at 12 per cent moisture content and d is nail diameter in mm. The subscripts signify as follows: gi, green immediate withdrawal; gd, green delayed; di, dry immediate; and dd, dry delayed.

The original test from which these equations have been derived was written for a nail of 2.8 mm diameter and the nail diameter was not included in those equations.

The delayed and immediate resistances are related as follows:

$$R_{gd} = 6.7\, R_{gi}{}^{0.90}$$

$$R_{dd} = 1.5\, R_{di}{}^{0.90}$$

The performance of nails with deformed shanks and polymer coatings under withdrawal loads is not as comprehensively established for the range of densities and timber conditions as indicated for plain nails. However, some useful general principles can be applied:

(a) For dry hardwoods of medium density and softwoods, polymer-coated and/or treated nails and nails with deformed shanks produce 1.7 to 2.0 times the withdrawal resistance of plain nails after three months delayed withdrawal;

(b) For green hardwoods, polymer-coated and -treated nails at three months delay have a similar performance to plain nails, while deformed shank nails have 1.7-2.0 times the withdrawal resistance of plain nails;

(c) For dry hardwoods of higher densities, e.g. jarrah and E. diversicolor, polymer coatings do not improve withdrawal resistance above that measured for plain nails.

3. Withdrawal resistance of nails

For plain and coated nails in dry timber, the displacement of the nail at ultimate load may be related to the shear properties of the timber and the withdrawal load may be related to the frictional properties of the nail and the timber. After initial failure, the total area of nail in contact with the wood is decreased, and it may be assumed that the coefficient of friction is also modified after the initial slip. Because the load-displacement or slip is dependent on wood properties, for dry timber the conventional relationship between shortand long-term strength properties might be expected to apply. That is, short-term properties will be approximately 1.5 times those measured after about three months. This is not in complete agreement with data shown for dry material.

For wood nailed green and allowed to dry, particularly hardwood species, the wood can be expected to shrink up to 10 per cent and there may be splitting and deterioration of the wood around the nail. These two actions, shrinkage and the accompanying loss of strength, can lead to variable results. This precludes a rational explanation of long-term behaviour in relation to measurements taken shortly after driving.

Working loads are not derived in this chapter, but in general they will be approximately one quarter of the maximum value.

The withdrawal resistance of nails driven into the end grain is the subject of current research, which tends to show that end-grain loads are 0.5-0.7 of the side-grain loads. However, present code stipulations allow no load to be assigned to nails driven into the end grain.

End and edge distances for nails in withdrawal are discussed in the relevant design codes.

4. Load-deflection curve for screw withdrawal

Figure 17 shows the withdrawal force-displacement for a 5.6 mm shank diameter, mild steel screw driven into a dry hardwood (jarrah) of 850 kg/m^3 density.

Figure 17. Load-displacement curves for 5.6 mm diameter wood screw with (A) one loading and (B) two loadings

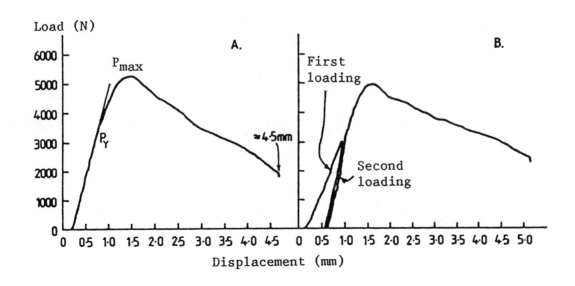

First, a characteristic settling in occurs. Thereafter, the load-displacement relationship is linear almost up to the maximum load. Where the load is cycled, the second and subsequent loads produce a stiffer joint than the first load. Wood elements located between the threads of the screw are loaded in shear and bending and the behaviour of the fastener is compatible with the elastic deformation of these annular elements.

This elastic displacement, 2 mm, is greater than that encountered with nails where the slip is related directly to the embedded length and the shear modulus of the wood.

After 2.5 mm displacement, the load on the screw remains at a relatively high level and thereafter decreases, like the withdrawal load on a nail. This behaviour is in line with a resistance determined by friction and a decreasing area of sheared wood.

5. Maximum screw withdrawal loads

The same source that provided data for nail withdrawal yields similar equations for screws. For steel screws driven into the side grain of wood, the equations shown in table 3 can be used:

Table 3. Screw withdrawal resistance and density

Initial moisture content of timber	Time of test	Regression between withdrawal resistance R (N) and density D (kg/m^3) [a]
Green	Immediate	$R_{gi} = 0.008\ D_b{}^{1.2}d$
	Three month delay before test	$R_{gd} = 0.018\ D_b{}^{1.1}d$
Dry	Immediate	$R_{di} = 0.014\ D_d{}^{1.2}d$
	Three month delay before test	$R_{dd} = 0.016\ D_d{}^{1.2}d$

[a] D_b is basic density, D_d is air-dry density at 12 per cent moisture content and d is screw diameter in mm. The subscripts signify as follows: gi, green immediate withdrawal; gd, green delayed; di, dry immediate; and dd, dry delayed.

The shank diameters over which these equations can be taken to apply range from 2.74 to 7.72 mm or from size 4 to size 18. Pre-drilling to the root diameter of the screw over its full length and a lead hole of the same diameter as the shank are required.

6. Withdrawal resistance of screws

The behaviour of hand-driven wood screws in withdrawal is different from that of nails because friction between the fastener and wood is not a major component of the resistance.

The equations for R_{di} and R_{dd} are not statistically different, although two separate equations are quoted, and R_{gd} is greater than R_{gi}, unlike the situation for nails, where the withdrawal resistance generally decreases with time. This may be explained by the contraction of the wood around the screw, which overrides any decrease in friction or deterioration in the physical properties of the wood.

Withdrawal loads for screws are roughly two to three times those for nails of similar diameter and penetration.

In codes, basic or working loads are normally subject to factoring for duration of loading, and two thirds of the value allowed for side grain can be applied to end grain.

The data are specific for pre-bored lead holes and are not applicable to self-tapping, machine-driven screws.

7. Lateral load-displacement curve for nailed joints

A typical load-displacement or slip curve is shown in figure 18 for a nail in single shear where an initial clearance exists between the members, i.e. friction in the joints is not included in the initial load. The relationship between load and slip is curvilinear over its entire range, and numerous approaches, ranging from the empirical to the fundamental, have been made to analyse the curve and predict loads.

Figure 18. Typical load-slip curve for a 75 mm x 2.8 mm diameter nail in single shear loaded parallel to grain

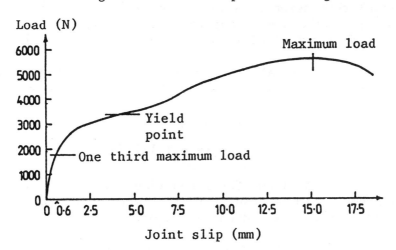

Mack's analyses of nailed joints [2, 3, 4] led to an equation where, for a nail diameter d, the load P (in N) up to a limiting joint displacement δ of 2.5 mm was given by the following equation:

$$P_{2.5} = 0.165 \ d^{1.75} M(0.128\delta + 0.68)(1 - e^{-3\delta})^{0.56} \tag{1}$$

M in this equation can be regarded as a stiffness modulus or a factor characteristic of the species and moisture content.

The equation applies over the range $0 < \delta < 2.5$ but has limited application in the above form. It can be simplified up to slip values of 0.5 mm, giving

10 per cent higher values of load, by the following two equations (the first for green timber, the second for dry timber), which apply to a single loading in a 5-min test:

$$P_{0.5g} = 0.023 \ d^{1.75}D_b^{1.4}\delta^{0.5}$$

$$P_{0.5d} = 0.135 \ d^{1.75}D_d^{1.1}\delta^{0.5}$$

where D_b and D_d are the basic and air-dry densities in kg/m^3 and $P_{0.5}$ signifies that the relationship holds up to about 0.5 mm slip with the accuracy stated.

A change in curvature occurs at between 50 and 60 per cent of the maximum load; this is referred to loosely as the yield point. Working loads are roughly one sixth to one third of ultimate loads, so that the initial slip at the working load may be about 0.10-0.5 mm depending on nail diameter, timber density and initial moisture content.

There is no linear portion of the curve in the initial stages of loading, although some workers define short and long-term stiffness moduli that assume an initial linear range. The equations presented are used as a basis for calculating long- and short-term deformations in the Australian Timber Engineering Code [5] for a range of densities.

Because working loads for nails are well below the yield point, analyses of the load-slip curve up to about 1.0 mm slip are relevant in establishing design information, and a 10 per cent accuracy is probably acceptable.

8. Ultimate load capacity of laterally loaded nails

The empirical regression equations of Mack [4] produce loads comparable to those obtained from either semi-empirical studies such as those of Moller [6] and Meyer [7] or empirical studies such as those of Brock [8] and Morris [9].

Mack's equations correlate well over a wide range of timber densities. For one nail in single shear in a three-member joint, they are as follows:

$$P_g = 0.3 \ D_b^{1.1}d^{1.75}$$

$$P_d = 0.17 \ D_d^{1.1}d^{1.75}$$

where P_g is the ultimate load for green timber in N, D_d is the basic density in kg/m^3, P_d is the ultimate load for dry timber in N, D_d is the air-dry density in kg/m^3 and d is the nail diameter in mm.

Similar equations are quoted by Mack for loads at 0.4 mm slip. The equations in the test from which these were derived were specific to 2.8 mm diameter nails, and the above relationships use a dependency of load on nail diameter to the power 1.75.

This result is somewhat different from the results for other equations for load capacity, where load is related to diameter squared and is also taken to be directly related to density.

For instance, Brock's equation would be

$$P_d = 0.26 \ D_d d^2$$

It produces a result comparable to that of Mack's equation; working loads are based on one third of the maximum load derived by this formula, which relates to dry timber.

It is worth noting the basis used by Moller, and later refined by Meyer [7], to determine the lateral load capacity: both the bending of the nail in a joint and the bearing stress on the wood were taken into account to produce the following equation:

$$P = kd^2 \sqrt{f_n f_c}$$

where P is the maximum load, d is the nail diameter, f_n is the ultimate stress in bending of the nail (the plastic modulus is used), f_c is the maximum rod-bearing strength of wood and k is a numerical constant.

This equation accurately predicts test results at the yield point but underestimates failure loads [2]. To take account of nail deflection at higher levels of slip, where the nail tends to pull out of the wood, Meyer derived a "rope" stress. When added to Moller's load, the ultimate load was accurately predicted.

9. Deformation of laterally loaded nails

The prediction of slip in nailed joints can be important in design, e.g. for built-up beams where deflection is an important design consideration.

Either of the equations for $P_{0.5g}$ or $P_{0.5d}$ can be transposed to establish values of displacements up to 0.5 mm, i.e.

$$\delta = 36 \ (P/M)^2 (1/d^3)$$

Here M is the stiffness modulus, which is related to density by the following equation:

$$M_g = 0.14 \ D_b^{1.4}$$

or

$$M_d = 0.82 \ D_d^{1.1}$$

Where a load produces a slip in excess of 0.5 mm, but less than 2.5 mm, the slip value may be obtained by interpolation from the load at 2.5 mm $(P_{2.5})$, given by the following equation:

$$P_{2.5} = 0.165 \ d^{1.75} M$$

Values of slip calculated on the above basis are increased for various load durations and for initially green timber that dries under load.

10. Lateral load capacity of wood screws

A load-deformation curve for wood screws under lateral load is not presented nor is the slip of screwed joints discussed. The formula generally quoted for calculating the proportional limit lateral loads is derived from tests conducted at Cornell University in 1913 [10] and is given as follows:

$$P = Kd^2/145$$

Values of K vary from 3,300 to 6,400 for hardwoods and from 3,300 to 5,200 for softwoods of North American origin, and d is the screw shank diameter in mm. The data are relevant to dry wood.

The equation applies for a penetration of the screw into the receiving member of seven times the shank diameter with the lead hole drilled to 90 per cent of the root diameter. Pre-boring of the cleat or covering member to the shank diameter is required.

Basic loads are 0.63 of the proportional limit loads, and values of K quoted in the Wood Handbook [11] are relevant to basic loads.

Where penetration is less than seven diameters, the basic loads are reduced proportionally.

11. Lateral load capacity of wood screws

As screws under lateral loads may reasonably be regarded as an alternative to laterally loaded nails, the relevant behaviours of the two fasteners are worth comparing.

The data for nails under lateral loads related to joints where there was an initial clearance, and at low loads friction between the members was not important. With screwed joints, there would be initial friction. At the higher loads, a nail tends to withdraw from one member, while with a screwed joint a higher withdrawal load, and consequently a higher maximum load, may be expected.

Because of such considerations, the maximum lateral loads for nails and screws of the same diameter will differ as with the basic or design loads. It is of interest to note that allowable loads for nails and screws calculated from sources such as the Wood Handbook or from standard codes, e.g. AS 1720, have values of within 15-20 per cent of one another. Nail penetrations are greater than screw penetrations.

B. Bolted joints in wood

1. Load deformation characteristics of bolted joints

The load and displacement characteristics of bolted joints vary with species and bolt strength properties and with the thickness of members in relation to bolt diameter; in three-member joints, the material of the side plates is relevant.

An extensive empirical study by Trayer of three-member joints [12] showed that an initial linear relationship existed between load and joint slip. A proportional limit load was defined, and average proportional limit bearing stresses were determined for loading parallel and perpendicular to the grain. A range of widths of the centre member for a given bolt diameter and a limited range of species were covered.

A typical load displacement curve for a bolted joint may be of the form shown in figure 19 and the variation of proportional limit stress for a range of b/d ratios, where b is member thickness and d is bolt diameter, is also plotted in figure 20.

Figure 19. Typical load-slip curve for a bolted joint

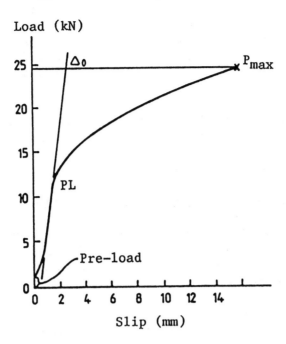

Figure 20. Variation of stress at the limit of
proportionality with b/d ratio

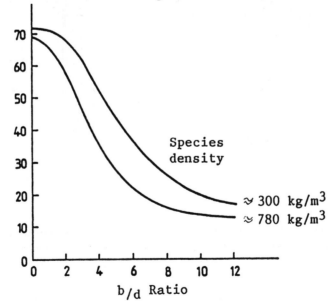

The displacement Δ_0 is an arbitrary value defined by the slope of the linear section and its intersection with a horizontal line through the maximum load.

While Trayer's work has formed the basis of a number of current timber design codes, more recent investigations [13, 14] have shown that the linear relationship may not always be obtained and that the decrease in the proportional limit stress with increasing b/d ratio is different from that found in earlier work. The further application of Trayer's data to a range of species is limited by the absence of a basic analysis or a specific relationship between the proportional limit stress, bolt diameter and timber properties such as density, maximum crushing strength and compressive proportional limit stress.

The following section uses data from Mack that encompass a useful density range, as well as Trayer's information, to obtain an empirical relationship between bearing stress, timber and joint properties. A simplified version of Moller's theory is used to derive loads.

2. Determination of loads for bolted timber joints

The equations presented are relevant to a basic joint shown in figure 21; this is a three-member assembly in which the thickness of the side members is at least half the thickness of the centre member, which is then regarded as the effective or most highly stressed component.

Figure 21. Two types of bolted timber joint

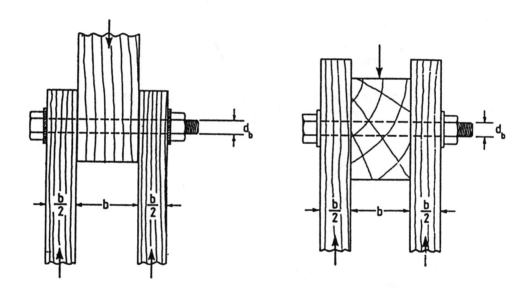

For a two member joint of equal thickness, the load capacity is about half that of the effective member of the same thickness in a three-piece assembly. For other joint configurations, loads can be derived accordingly.

In the equations that follow, the rod bearing stress f_c corresponds to the average proportional limit stress, determined by the proportional limit load P_L and the projected area of the bolt in the effective member. It is similar to the stress measured in a loading system as shown in figure 22 with a uniform load applied to the rod. It is not directly related to the basic timber properties in compression in these analyses.

Figure 22. Determination of rod bearing stress

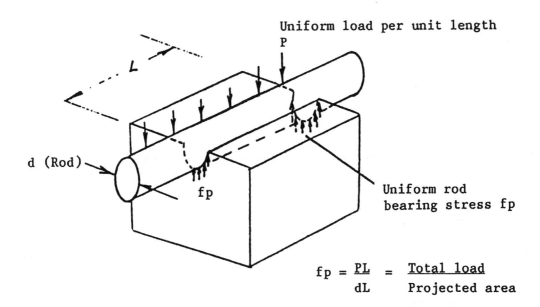

$$fp = \frac{PL}{dL} = \frac{\text{Total load}}{\text{Projected area}}$$

The rod bearing stress f_c differs with direction of loading. In a three-member assembly it is given by

(a) For green timber under loading parallel to grain,

$$f_c = 0.15 \, D_b^{0.75}$$

(b) For dry timber, parallel loading,

$$f_c = 0.24 \, D_d^{0.75}$$

(c) For green timber, loading perpendicular to grain,

$$f_c = \frac{1.0 \, D_b^{0.5}}{d^{0.5}}$$

(d) For dry timber, perpendicular loading,

$$f_c = \frac{1.6 \, D_b^{0.5}}{d^{0.5}}$$

Loads at the limit of proportionality, P_L, can be calculated using the above values of f_c on the following basis:

$$P_L \text{ is the lesser of } P_{(L1)} \text{ and } P_{(L2)}$$

where $P_{(L1)} = f_c bd$, $P_{(L2)} = 0.85 \, d^2 \sqrt{f_c f_y}$ for timber side and centre members and $P_{(L2)} = d^2 \sqrt{f_c f_y}$ for steel side and timber centre members.

The maximum load on the joint, P_{max}, is given by the following equations:

(a) Loading parallel to grain

$$P_{max} = 2f_c bd$$

(b) Perpendicular loading

$$P_{max} = 4f_c bd$$

In each of the above equations, the relevant value of f_c is to be calculated for use in determining the load capacity for the particular loading pattern. The notation is as follows:

f_c = Nominal rod bearing stress (N)

f_y = Yield stress for bolts used in the joint (typically about 300 MPa for mild steel)

D_b = Basic density (kg/m^3)

D_d = Air-dry density (kg/m^3)

d = Bolt diameter (mm)

b = Effective member thickness (mm)

P_L = Proportional limit load (kN)

P_{max} = Maximum load on joint (kN)

3. Slip in bolted joints

The following relationships serve for determining joint stiffness in kN/mm:

S = 0.6 P_{max} for joints loaded either parallel or perpendicular to the grain in green and dry timber

S' = 1.5 P_{max} for three-member assemblies with steel side plates

4. Load capacity of bolted joints

The above equations are compatible with the existing empirical and theoretical data on bolted joints. At b/d ratios of less than about 4, a uniform stress exists under the bolt, and timber properties determine loads at the proportional limit. With increasing b/d, the deflection of the bolt becomes more important; higher bearing stresses at the edge of the effective member are developed, with a resulting decrease in the average rod bearing stress. Thus, at higher b/d ratios the yield strength of the bolt becomes important in determining the yield load.

At maximum load, available data suggest that the variation in stress under the bolt with increasing b/d is less than occurs with the load at proportional limit. The maximum load can be regarded as being determined mainly by the wood bearing properties.

Trayer found that the stress remained constant at some proportion of the maximum crushing stress for parallel loading, although the Malaysian work [14] shows some decrease with increasing b/d, particularly under parallel loadings.

5. Practical aspects of bolted joint design

The spacing of bolts for end and edge distances in both tensile and compression loading and the distance between parallel rows of bolts were established or specified by Trayer and are still applied.

These recommendations were as follows:

(a) Centre to centre spacings of at least four times bolt diameter parallel to the grain, regardless of b/d ratio;

(b) Spacing of approximately 80 per cent of the total area under bearing of all the bolts in the joint;

(c) End margin for compression loading the same as bolt spacing, namely four times bolt diameter, measured to the centre of the bolt;

(d) Under tension loads, an end distance of at least seven diameters;

(e) For loads perpendicular to the grain, the spacing across the grain needs only to permit tightening of the bolt. Between-bolt spacings along the grain are dependent on b/d values; for b/d > 6, spacings of at least five diameters are required;

(f) For seasoned material, the clearance between bolts and holes was minimal in Trayer's analysis, but where joints of green material were assembled and then allowed to air dry, the load capacity decreased substantially; proportional limit loads ranged from 25 to 40 per cent of what was expected where loading was carried out directly after assembly. Where bolts are used for green hardwoods that have high (e.g. 10%) shrinkage, clearances of the same order may be necessary to obviate splitting, and allowances should be proportional to bolt diameters. Where joint slip is important, the extra clearance must be accommodated owing to the ovality of the hole;

(g) Washers should be used under the heads and nuts on bolted joints, but the optimal size is a matter of some conjecture. For the diameters of bolts in common use, e.g. 10 and 12 mm, maximum washer sizes of 50 x 50 x 3 mm have been suggested.

C. Split ring and shear plate connectors

1. Load deformation characteristics

Figures 23 and 24 show typical load deformation curves for two split rings in a three-member compression joint, two shear plates in a three-member compression joint and two shear plates in a three-member tension joint.

Figure 23. Load-slip curve for 2 x 102 mm split rings,
initial load range expanded

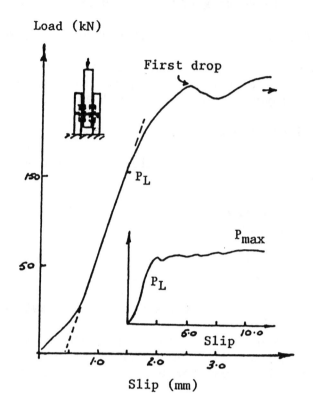

When loaded in compression, the behaviour of these connectors is similar to that of bolted joints. Some observed differences are a well-defined initial setting in deformation with shear plates and for both shear plates and split rings, a primary failure occurs in advance of the maximum failure load.

With shear plate connections, clearance between the bolt and the pilot hole can affect the initial deformation. The load is transmitted in the early loading phase through the bolt to the adjoining member, and where the hole in the wood is smaller than that in the connector, the initial slip may be relatively large.

The primary failure observed in both types of connector under compression loading is regarded as a shear failure of the central core of the wood encompassed by the connector. Final failure is due to compression failure of the wood around the peripheral surface of the plate or ring.

In tension tests on shear plates, failure occurs when a split develops owing to the lateral force exerted by the plate. The slip is less at failure under tension loads than under compression loads.

Figure 24.   Load—slip curves for 2 x 104 mm shear plates in
90 mm thick Douglas fir with steel side plates

Total load on joint (kN)

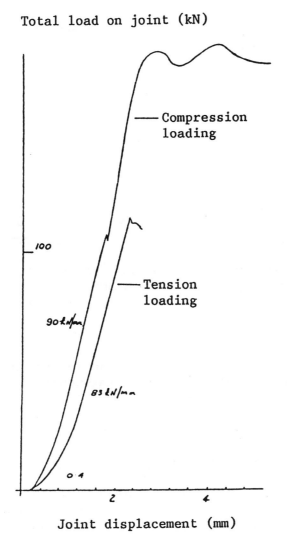

Joint displacement (mm)

2.   Determination of basic loads

For split rings, a number of sources [15, 16, 17] indicate that maximum
loads and proportional limit loads can be expressed empirically as follows:

$$P = kD$$

where P is the relevant load expressed either as P_{max}, the maximum load, or
P_L, the proportional limit load, in kN; D is either the basic density D_b
or the air-dry density D_d, in kg/m³; and k is taken from the relationships
shown in table 4 [17].

Information directly relevant to shear plates is less well documented,
but for a single 102 mm plate with a 24 mm bolt in compression parallel to the
grain, the following equation may be applicable:

$$P_{max} = 0.14 \ D_b$$

Table 4. Empirical relationships between load and density
for split rings a/

| Split rings | Direction of load to grain | Moisture content of the wood | $P = kD$ | |
			P_L	P_{max}
64 mm dia., 12 mm bolt	Parallel	Green	$0.04\ D_b$	$0.087\ D_b$
		Dry	$0.046\ D_d$	$0.093\ D_d$
	Perpendicular	Green	$0.024\ D_b$	$0.037\ D_b$
		Dry	$0.027\ D_d$	$0.042\ D_d$
102 mm dia., 20 mm bolt	Parallel	Green	$0.087\ D_b$	$0.16\ D_b$
		Dry	$0.094\ D_d$	$0.17\ D_d$
	Perpendicular	Green	$0.048\ D_b$	$0.070\ D_b$
		Dry	$0.054\ D_d$	$0.085\ D_d$

a/ The load per ring or connector as quoted is half the total load applied to the centre member of a three-member assembly. The values of P_L and P_M are approximately half those tabulated in the work from which the data were derived.

Limited work on the measurement of loads in tension parallel to the grain for 102 mm plates suggests that, in green hardwoods and dry conifers, the following equation holds for one plate:

$$P_{max} = 0.055\ D_b$$

3. Slip in split ring and shear plate joints

Slip in the linear range is determined from the proportional limit load and the corresponding displacement. Since there is no established theoretical basis for relating the performance of different diameters, the relationships are empirical.

As load is directly related to density, joint stiffness can be defined in terms of density of the timber in the joint for a given diameter of ring. The relevant relationships are shown in table 5.

Table 5. Stiffness for three-member joint with two split rings

| Split ring diameter (mm) | Moisture content of the wood | Stiffness (kN/mm) a/ | |
		Load parallel to grain	Load perpendicular to grain
102	Green and dry	$0.15\ D_{b,d}$	$0.06\ D_{b,d}$
64	Green and dry	$0.07\ D_{b,d}$	$0.03\ D_{b,d}$

a/ The subscript in the term $D_{b,d}$ refers to basic or air-dry density.

Slip δ at load P, where P $<$ P_L, is given by the following:

$$\delta_P = P/\text{stiffness}$$

4. Split rings and shear plate performance

The load capacity of split rings and shear plates is determined by both the shear and compression strengths of the wood. Since such properties are related to density, a correlation between load capacity and density can be expected.

The 64 mm split ring has approximately half the load capacity of the 102 mm ring, with about the same slip at the proportional limit. The stiffness of the smaller ring may reasonably be taken to be half that of the larger.

Data on shear plates are not extensive, but the general similarity between their behaviour and that of split rings and the accordance between the results available for both types of connectors suggest that the performance of a shear plate may be predicted by a set of equations similar to that given for split rings.

With green hardwoods, particularly near the ends of a tension member, split rings are preferred to shear plates because they can accommodate shrinkage of the wood.

D. Tooth plate connectors

1. Load-deformation curve

The load-slip characteristics of a metal tooth plate connector in tension parallel to the punched slots are shown in figure 25. The relationship is curvilinear over the load range and more closely resembles the lateral load displacement of a nail joint in shear rather than that of a bolted or a shear plate connector joint. There is no well-defined yield load.

Where the load corresponding to a displacement of 2.5 mm is designated by $P_{2.5}$ and the load at a slip δ mm by P_δ, the ratio of loads is given by

$$\frac{P_\delta}{P_{2.5}} = (0.13\delta + 0.68)(1 - e^{-3\delta})^{0.7}$$

This form of the relationship is very similar to the reduced load equation for nailed joints and was established for 14- and 18-gauge plates and two species. It is of limited value because $P_{2.5}$ is generally not known in terms of the maximum load on the joint.

The empirical relationship for two types of 20-gauge plates in two dry softwood species, based on maximum load (P_{max}), may be stated as follows:

$$\frac{P_\delta}{P_{max}} = 1.25\,\delta^{0.7}$$

This applies up to $P_\delta/P_{max} = 0.6$ and covers a useful range since joint design loads are generally 30 per cent of the maximum load carried on the joint. With the knowledge of an experimentally determined P_{max}, values of δ at design loads may be obtained.

Figure 25. Typical load-slip curve for a metal-toothed, 2 x 1 mm
thick plate connector in softwood

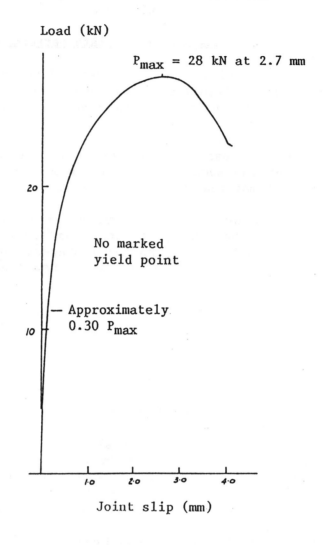

Load (kN)

P_{max} = 28 kN at 2.7 mm

No marked
yield point

— Approximately
0.30 P_{max}

Joint slip (mm)

2. Load capacity of joints

Because of the diversity of tooth shapes, plate thicknesses and plate
dimensions, there is no single relationship encompassing all types of connector, between connector strength, wood properties and plate orientations and
specifications.

For a given design of plate and particular configuration of width and
length, the maximum load capacity of one plate in tension parallel to the
punched slots may be expressed as follows:

$$P_{max} = knpD$$

$$P_{max} \leq lf$$

where P_{max} is the maximum load capacity of one plate in N, k is an empirical
constant for the plate, n is the effective number of teeth acting on one plate
on one side of a joint, p is the manufacturer's experimentally determined

maximum load per tooth, D is the density of the timber in kg/m^3, 1 is the width of plate in mm and f is the manufacturer's experimentally determined maximum load per unit width of plate.

Thus, at the current time the load capacity of nail plates is based on experimentally determined data, and joint design relies on the application of manufacturers' recommended loads. Different values of load per tooth are quoted for a variety of loading situations and are considered to be directly related to timber density up to a limiting value where metal properties determine the maximum load.

3. Performance of tooth plate connectors

Investigations have shown that for a given species, the load per tooth in tension has a high correlation with wood density up to a load condition where the tensile strength of the plate across the perforations is reached; above this value, the load remains constant. For different species, e.g. two soft-woods, the relationship between load per tooth and density will lie along two different curves (figure 26). However, it is considered that a plot of species mean densities vs. load per tooth for a particular plate will show a linear relationship (figure 27) and the general dependency of load capacity on wood density is justified.

Figure 26. Load/tooth-density relationships at maximum load for toothed 20-gauge plate connectors in radiata pine and spruce

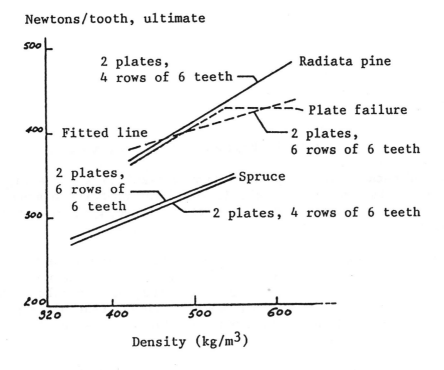

At the highest wood densities, there may be either plate failure or, for heavy gauge plates, shear failure at the root of the teeth (rather than tooth withdrawal). Incomplete penetration of the plate tooth into wood of high density may lead to an anomalous behaviour.

Figure 27. Load/tooth-mean density relationship for a toothed
plate connector

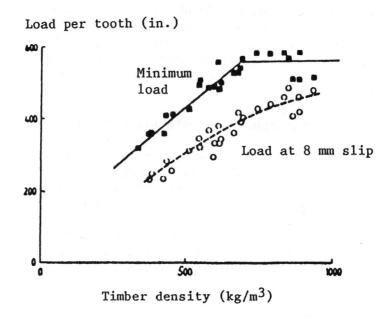

E. <u>Metal support brackets or framing anchors</u>

A range of metal brackets pressed from galvanized steel strip or plate of
1.2 mm (18-gauge) thickness is available for jointing between studs and plates,
plates and rafters, trusses and plates etc. Three typical applications are
shown in figure 28.

Experimental investigation of the load-deformation behaviour of brackets
tested either singly or in pairs in a seasoned softwood shows a curved relationship (figure 29) with failure occurring either as a result of timber fracture or through buckling of the steel member. Timber fracture can result where
nails are placed in the bracket adjacent to a timber edge and loads are applied
perpendicular to the grain.

An important use of such brackets is in housing construction in situations
where deformations of a few millimeters may be permissible, e.g. in connecting
internal walls to the underside of roof trusses, with joints between hanging
beams and ceiling joists. The stiffness of the components in these applications is probably not critical, and load capacities should not therefore be
based on arbitrarily low slip values.

The geometry of the various anchors, brackets and straps is complex, and load capacities vary with the direction of the applied load. It is not possible, therefore, to rationally develop load capacity at this stage, and the simple addition of the lateral and/or withdrawal load capacities of the nails in the joints may overestimate the total capacity.

As with tooth plate connectors, the use of sheet metal framing connectors relies on the provision of adequate design data by the manufacturers. For the fasteners to be adapted to a specific situation the design data must be relevant to the situation.

Figure 28.   Typical applications of metal brackets in jointing
timber members

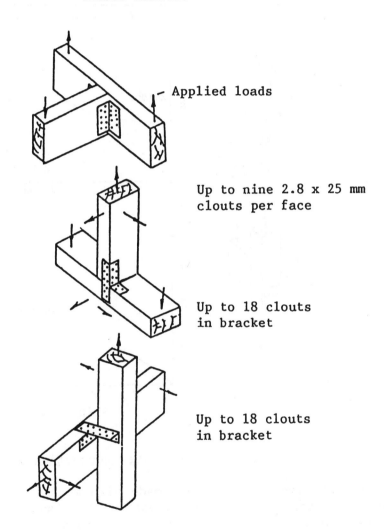

Figure 29. Load-deformation behaviour of joints formed with metal
brackets, softwood having a density of 450-500 kg/m³

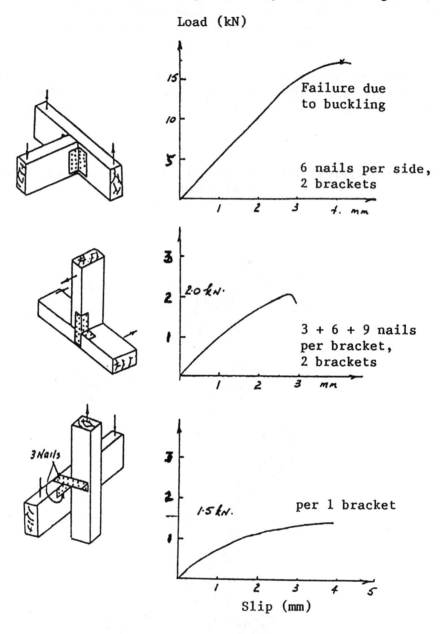

F. Costs of timber connections

The cost of timber connections made with mechanical fasteners can simply
be estimated in terms of the unit cost of the fasteners involved. Such an
approach may, however, have little or no relevance to the overall cost of the
component in place in a structure. This overall cost will be determined by a
number of other factors that need to be assessed for the particular application.

The most basic mechanical fastener, the hand-driven plain wire nail used
in lightly loaded structures such as domestic dwellings, is the cheapest method
of connecting members in cases where the following are true:

(a) Cheap scantling such as green hardwood can be cut and nailed in
on-site construction;

(b) Labour skilled in this method of construction is available;

(c) Dwellings are built in relatively small numbers in specific localities.

This has been the typical pattern of building in certain areas, e.g. the Melbourne metropolitan area, and where pre-cutting and assembly off-site cannot compete with the hand-cutting, assembly and hand-nailing of relatively short runs of a particular house design.

In other areas, where skilled labour is not as readily available and generally similar dwelling designs can be duplicated in estates of relatively large numbers of houses, different cost criteria apply. There, higher rates of productivity can be achieved on repetitive operations, and the higher unit cost of connectors, together with the costs of cartage between factory and site and on-site assembly, is offset by lower labour costs.

The in-place cost of a gun-driven nail or a pressed nail plate can therefore be competitive with the cost of several hand-driven nails in a joint if production rates are sufficiently high.

In general, the load capacity of many bolted joints can be achieved with a nail plate of suitable gauge and dimensions. In truss fabrication, the setting up of members and pressing of the plate, even for a relatively short production run, can be carried out at lower cost than the fabricating of a bolted joint of equal load capacity. The bolt hole has to be located, generally in three intersecting members, the hole drilled and the bolt fitted and tightened. A metal splice plate may also be required with attendant dimensioning, drilling and fitting.

On the basis of cost alone, there would appear to be limited justification for bolted joints in the normal size range of commercial trusses. An added, perhaps ill-defined cost exists, however, in terms of aesthetics, and some architects and designers specify a bolted joint in preference to a nail plate. The added cost of the bolt may be substantial, but it is preferred for reasons not directly related to monetary considerations.

Where bolts are used in conjunction with shear plates and split rings, the load capacity of the joint is increased so that fewer structural elements will be necessary to carry a given total load. With such connectors, the increased capacity is obtained at a total economic cost made up by the following:

(a) Selection and marking out of timber;
(b) Drilling and grooving timber;
(c) Fitting the connector;
(d) Assembling the structure;
(e) The cost of a bolt and connectors.

Some industrial experience shows that a bolt and split ring connected truss with steel gusset plates may cost 20 times as much as a nail plate connected truss of the same span, but at a lesser spacing. The main difference in cost comes from the additional labour associated with multiple handling of the timber and longer assembly times.

Table 6 lists Australian prices in 1983 for various fasteners and estimates the cost of these fasteners in place in a structure. Machining and handling times have been based partly on estimates and partly on known or measured production times. Labour has been costed at $A 15 per hour. It is not possible to arrive at a consistent basis for comparing the various connectors; the footnotes to the table indicate the different bases of the costs.

Table 6. Estimated cost of timber connectors

Item	Size (mm) a/	A unit cost ($A)	B Estimated fabrication time b/	Cost in place A + B + extra ($A)
Hand-driven wire nails c/	3.75d x 75	0.006	5 sec	0.026
	2.8d x 75	0.0025	4 sec	0.019
Auto-machine-driven nails c/				
Polymer-coated	3.08d x 75	0.013	1.25 sec	0.018
Helically grooved	3.08d x 75	0.020	1.25 sec	0.025
Ring shank	3.08d x 75	0.020	1.25 sec	0.025
Framing anchors				
General-purpose saddle	–	0.25	2 min d/	0.75
Cyclone strap	–	0.22	2 min	0.72
Truss boot	–	4–5	5 min e/	5.00–6.00
Bolted joints (galvanized)	180 x 12d	1.05	10 min f/	3.55
	x 16d	1.70	10 min	4.20
	x 20d	2.54	10 min	5.00
Nail plates	75 x 100 x 1.0	0.20	6 sec g/	0.20 + 0.12 +0.05 = 0.37
Shear plates (2)) two–	108d + 24d	2 x 3.75 (+ 4.74)	15 min	15.95
+ bolt)member	68d + 20d	2 x 1.64 (+ 2.54)	15 min	9.54
Split ring)joint	102d + 20d	1.14 (+ 2.54)	15 min	7.40
+ bolt)	64d + 12d	0.72 (+ 1.05)	15 min	5.50

a/ Diameter is indicated by d.
b/ The estimated fabrication time in some cases includes an assembly time as well as the time needed to drive or fit the connector.
c/ The fabrication times are for driving the nails and do not include member placement.
d/ The framing anchor is assumed to be held by six cloutnails, and the time is that required for driving these fasteners.
e/ The truss boot is assumed to be held by two bolts.
f/ Fabrication time has been based on marking out, drilling and fitting the bolt to a final assembly. The time required to select and cut the timber is not included.
g/ The in-place cost includes amortization and interest changes on a plant costing $A 80,000 and a production rate of 200 trusses per day, using four operators (at $A 18/hr) and 20 plates per truss. Time includes laying up of the truss.

G. Summary

A basis has been provided, where adequate theory or empirical data exist, for calculating the maximum or proportional limit loads for a range of timber fasteners in common use. The geometry and behaviour under load of tooth plate connectors and pressed metal framing anchors is complex. Experimentally derived performance data provide the best basis for determining load capabilities for these fasteners.

The derivation of design loads from maximum or proportional limit loads requires the application of a load factor, which varies with area of use and type of load. Such factors are not derived in this chapter.

The short discussion of costs shows that accurate determinations would require detailed work studies, which would be available to experienced industry fabricators. Some general assessments are possible and the data can be modified if the fabrication times or details seem inappropriate. There is a large cost difference between nail plate and bolt connector methods of jointing.

References

1. J. J. Mack, "The withdrawal resistance of plain steel nails and screws in Australian timber", Technical Paper (Second Series) No. 30 (Melbourne, CSIRO, Division of Building Research, 1979).

2. J. J. Mack, "The strength and stiffness of nailed joints under short-duration loading", Technical Paper No. 40 (Melbourne, CSIRO, Division of Building Research, 1966).

3. J. J. Mack, "The load-displacement curve for nailed joints", Journal of the Institute of Wood Science, vol. 7, No. 6 (1977), pp. 34-36.

4. J. J. Mack, "The establishment of lateral working loads for nailed joints for Australian conditions", Technical Paper (Second Series) No. 27 (Melbourne, CSIRO, Division of Building Research, 1978).

5. Standards Association of Australia, Australian Standard 1720-1975: SAA Timber Engineering Code (Sydney, 1975).

6. T. Moller, "En ny metod for bera kning av spikforband (New method of estimating the bearing strength of nailed connections)", Sweden Handlingar Nr 117 (Goteborg, Chalmers Tekniska Hogskolas, 1951).

7. A. Meyer, "Die Tragfaehigkeit von Nagelverbindungen bei statischer Belastung (The bearing strength of nailed joints under static load)", Holz als Rohund Werkstoff, vol. 15, No. 2 (1957), pp. 96-109.

8. G. R. Brock, "The strength of nailed joints", Forest Products Research Bulletin, No. 41, 1957.

9. E. N. Morris, "The application of slip-modulus in the design of nailed joints", Journal of the Institute of Wood Science, vol. 6, No. 2 (1973), pp. 17-21.

10. A. Kolberk and M. Birnkaum, "Transverse strength of screws in wood", Cornell Civil Engineering, No. 22, 1913, pp. 31-41.

11. United States Department of Agriculture, Forest Products Laboratory, Wood Handbook, No. 72 (Washington, D.C., 1955).

12. G. W. Trayer, "The bearing strength of wood under bolts", Technical Bulletin No. 332 (Madison, Wisconsin, United States Department of Agriculture, 1932).

13. J. J. Mack, "The strength of bolted joints in Australian timbers", Technical Paper (Second Series) No. 45 (Melbourne, CSIRO, Division of Building Research, 1978).

14. Chu Yue Pun, "Strength of bolted joints", Malaysian Forester, vol. 43, No. 1 (1980), pp. 88-115.

15. J. A. Scholten, "Timber-connector joints – their strength and design", Technical Bulletin No. 865 (Madison, Wisconsin, United States Department of Agriculture, 1944).

16. J. J. Mack, "Split-ring and shear plate connector joints in some Australian timbers", Technical Paper (Second Series) No. 41 (Melbourne, CSIRO, Division of Building Research, 1981).

17. Chu Yue Pun, "Strength of split-ring connectored joints", Malaysian Forester, vol. 42, No. 2 (1979), pp. 45-164.

Bibliography

Ehlbeck, J. Nailed joints in wood structures. No. 166. Virginia, Polytechnical Institute and State University, Wood Research and Wood Construction Laboratory, September 1979.

Johansen, K. W. Theory of timber connectors. Publication 9. Zurich, Switzerland, International Association for Bridge and Structural Engineering, 1949, pp. 249-262.

Mack, J. J. The strength of nailed joints, I. In messmate stringbark. Technological Paper No. 9. South Melbourne, CSIRO, Division of Forest Products, 1960.

National Forest Products Association. Natural design specification for stress grade lumber and its fastenings. Washington, D.C., 1973.

Thomas, K. Mechanical fasteners. Structural engineer (London) 60A:2, February 1982.

Vermeyden, P. Tests on bolted joints. Report 4-80-1, Onderzoek B2. Delft, Netherlands, Technische Hogeschool, Steven – Laboratorium Houtconstructies, 1980.

III. BUCKLING STRENGTH OF TIMBER COLUMNS AND BEAMS

Robert H. Leicester*

Introduction

The effects of slenderness on the strength of timber structures are frequently of considerable practical significance. However, it is usually difficult to write effective design rules to cope with these effects, because while these rules must be simple for practical purposes, their applications are extremely varied. This difficulty is compounded by the lack of adequate theoretical and experimental information and by the large number of parameters that affect buckling strength.

This chapter describes simple models for the buckling strength of columns and beams and indicates how these may be applied in the formulation of design codes. The method is generalized for more complex cases. The analysis of the structures with buckling restraints will also be discussed briefly.

The following notation is used in this chapter:

A	= Area
a_{bo}, a_{co}	= Crookedness parameters, equations (48) and (31)
b	= Width of cross-section
d	= Depth of cross-section
E	= Modulus of elasticity
F	= Stress capacity of stable members
F_{cr}	= Elastic buckling stress
F_c, F_b, F_t	= Allowable design values of compression, bending and tension stress for stable members
F_{cu}, F_{bu}	= Ultimate compression and bending stress of stable members
F_u	= Ultimate stress capacity of a stable member
f	= Applied stress
f_c, f_b, f_t	= Applied compression, bending and tension stress
f_{bx}	= Allowable applied bending stress for members that are bent only about the major or x-axis
f_{cx}, f_{cy}	= Allowable applied stress for columns that can buckle through bending only about the x-axis or y-axis, respectively

---

*An officer of CSIRO, Division of Building Research, Melbourne.

f_{bu}, f_{cu} = Applied ultimate bending and compression stress for members that are unstable

f_{bxu} = Applied ultimate bending stress for members that are bent only about the major or x-axis

f_{cxu}, f_{cyu} = Applied ultimate compression stress for members that can buckle through bending only about the x-axis or y-axis, respectively

f_u = Applied nominal stress at failure

$h(m)$ = A function of moisture content defined by equation (13)

I_x, I_y = Moments of inertia about the x- and y-axis, respectively

K_R = Stiffness of lateral restraint

k = Stability factor

k_{bx}, k_{cx}, k_{cy} = Stability factors for obtaining the allowable design stresses f_{bx}, f_{cx} and f_{cy}

k_{bxu}, k_{cxu}, k_{cyu} = Stability factors for obtaining the ultimate stress capacities f_{bxu}, f_{cxu} and f_{cyu}

k_u = Stability factor for obtaining the applied stress at failure f_u

1 = Length of column or span of beam

L_a = Distance between points of lateral restraint

M = Applied bending moment

M_{cr} = Elastic buckling moment

$M_{cr(x)}$ = Elastic buckling moment for applied moment that causes bending about the x-axis

M_D, M_T = Dead and total load components, respectively, of the applied ultimate moment

M_D', M_T' = Dead and total load components, respectively, of the allowable design moment

m = Moisture content

N = Number of lateral restraints

n = Wave number of eigenmode shape, equation (80)

P = Load, axial load

P_{cr} = Elastic buckling load on a column

$P_{cr(x)}$ = Elastic buckling load on a column that can buckle by bending about the x-axis only

$P_{cr(n)}$ = Estimated elastic buckling load for column with eigenmode shape with wave number n, equation (81)

P_D, P_T = Dead and total load components, respectively, of the applied ultimate load on a column

P_D', P_T' = Dead and total load components, respectively, of the allowable design load on a column

P_O = Elastic buckling load for a pin-ended column, equation (82)

P_R = Force on a lateral restraint

r_b = M_D/M_T, M_D'/M_T'

r_c = P_D/P_T, P_D'/P_T'

S = Slenderness coefficient

S_{bx} = Slenderness coefficient for a beam that is bent about the major or x-axis

S_{cx}, S_{cy} = Slenderness coefficient for a column that can buckle only through bending about its x- or y-axis, respectively

u,v = Total deformations in the x and y directions, respectively

u_s, v_s = Deformations that would remain after the load is removed

u_t = Deformation at the location of the t-th lateral restraint

x,y,z = Cartesian coordinates; x and y are the major and minor axes, respectively, and z is in the direction along the length of the beam or column, figure 32

Z_x, Z_y = Section modulus about the x- and y-axis, respectively

α = Stress amplification factor due to member slenderness

α_D, α_T = Value of α due to dead and total loads, respectively

Δ = Deflection or deformation

Δ_e = Elastic component of Δ

Δ_o = Initial value of Δ_s

Δ_s = Value of Δ that remains if the load is removed

ε = Strain

ε_e = Elastic component of ε

ε_o = Initial value of ε_s

ε_s = Value of ε that remains if the load is removed

η = Material parameter used in definition of slenderness, equation (8)

λ = Parameter indicating the magnitude of the load

λ_a = Value of λ for the applied load

λ_{cr} = Elastic buckling value of λ

λ_{cro} = Pseudo-elastic buckling value of λ, computed with the assumption that the buckling eigenmode has the same shape as the initial crookedness

ξ = Creep factor, equation (15)

ϕ = Twist rotation of an unstable beam

ϕ_o = Initial value of ϕ due to crookedness

χ = Slenderness parameter, equation (1)

Ω = Dimensionless restraint stiffness, equation (83)

A. Slenderness and stability factors

The large number of parameters that affect the buckling strength of timber structures may be divided roughly into two groups. The first contains those parameters that are usually specified as input parameters into the design process. These include the applied loads, the geometrical parameters of the structure and the basic structural properties of the timber such as its ultimate strength and stiffness. The second group of parameters that affect the buckling strength includes those that are usually not specified in the design process: member crookedness, material non-homogeneity and non-linear material characeristics.

To cope with the numerous parameters involved, two procedures are used:

(a) The specified parameters are combined to form two dimensionless numbers, the slenderness coefficient and the stability factor;

(b) Most of the unspecified parameters are ignored in modelling the structural behaviour, and the values of the remaining parameters are replaced by notional values chosen to fit the experimental data.

The most convenient definition of slenderness, denoted by χ, is

$$\chi = (F_u/F_{cr})^{1/2} \tag{1}$$

where F_u is the ultimate stress capacity of stable members and F_{cr} is the theoretical elastic buckling stress.

The stability factor is used to indicate the influence of slenderness or instability on strength. For the case of ultimate strength, the stability factor, denoted by K_u, is defined by

$$f_u = k_u F_u \qquad (2)$$

where f_u is the nominal applied stress at failure.

From equations (1) and (2) it is apparent that if the structural member is completely stable, then

$$k_u = 1 \qquad (3)$$

and if the ultimate strength is equal to the elastic buckling strength, then $f_u = F_{cr}$ and

$$k_u = 1/\chi^2 \qquad (4)$$

Equations (3) and (4), illustrated in figure 30A, represent upper bounds on the stability factor. The true values are lower than these bounds because of the influence of factors such as crookedness, creep and non-linear structural characteristics.

Figure 30. Effect of slenderness on strength

A. For slenderness coefficient X   B. For slenderness coefficient S

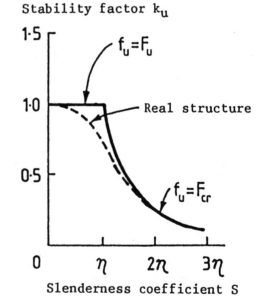

A more popular but less convenient definition of slenderness that is frequently used is

$$S = [(\pi^2/12)(E/F_{cu})(F_u/F_{cr})]^{1/2} \qquad (5)$$

where E is the modulus of elasticity parallel to the grain and F_{cu} is the ultimate compression strength. This definition is used because for the case of a pin-ended rectangular column it leads to the traditional definition

$$S = L/d \tag{6}$$

where L is the length of the column and d is the depth.

Note that equations (1) and (5) lead to

$$S = \eta \chi \tag{7}$$

where

$$\eta = [(\pi^2/12)(E/F_{cu})]^{1/2} \tag{8}$$

Thus, the equation for the case when the ultimate strength is equal to the buckling strength, $f_u = F_{cr}$, leads to

$$k_u = (\eta/S)^2 \tag{9}$$

Equation (9) is illustrated in figure 30B.

B. Creep deformations

Because lateral deformations lead to significant stresses in slender members, it is necessary to include the effects of creep in structural models of columns and beams. Information on rheological models of timber is scarce. The model used herein, illustrated schematically in figure 31, is based on the study by Leicester [1], [2].

Figure 31. Schematic representation of rheological model

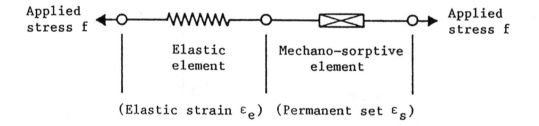

The basic unit of the model comprises an elastic and mechano-sorptive element connected in series. The total strain of the unit, denoted by , will be given by

$$\varepsilon = \varepsilon_s + \varepsilon_e \tag{10}$$

where ε_s and ε_e are the strains of the mechano-sorptive and elastic elements, respectively. The elastic element responds to an applied stress f in the usual manner:

$$\varepsilon_e = f/E \tag{11}$$

The strain of the mechano-sorptive element represents a permanent set that remains after the stress f is removed. It is changed when subjected to the combined influence of stress σ and a reduction in moisture content m during drying; the constitutive equation for this is

$$d\varepsilon_s/dm = -(f/E)h(m) \tag{12}$$

where h(m) is a positive function of moisture content.

Equation (12) may be written

$$d\varepsilon_s/dm = -\varepsilon_e h(m) \tag{13}$$

For the case of a member subjected to constant stress conditions, equation (13) leads to the following total strain ε after creep has taken place:

$$\varepsilon = \varepsilon_0 + \varepsilon_e(1 + \xi) \tag{14}$$

where ε_0 is the initial value of strain in the unstressed member and ξ, a creep factor, is given by

$$\xi = \int_{m2}^{m1} h(m)\, dm \tag{15}$$

Since the creep strains are directly proportional to the elastic strains, the deformation Δ of a simply supported beam is given by

$$\Delta = \Delta_0 + \Delta_e(1 + \xi) \tag{16}$$

where Δ_0 is the initial deformation of the unloaded beam and Δ_e is the elastic deformation due to the applied load.

The creep factor ξ for each given climate and duration regime is usually measured directly according to equation (16) rather than by attempting to evaluate it according to equation (15). For the life of typical structural elements, a value of $\xi = 1$ is usually used for initially dry timber and a value of $\xi = 2$ is taken for initially green timber.

In annex I the creep deformations of slender beams and columns are derived with the use of the rheological model described above.

C. Columns

1. General

For columns, the slenderness coefficient S_{cx}, defined by equation (5) for buckling about the x-axis, is given by

$$S_{cx} = (0.822\ EA/P_{cr(x)})^{1/2} \tag{17}$$

where A is the area of cross-section and $P_{cr(x)}$ is the elastic buckling column load for bending about the x-axis only.

The associated stability factor for buckling strength, denoted by k_{cxu}, is

$$f_{cxu} = k_{cxu}F_{cu} \tag{18}$$

where f_{cxu} is the applied axial stress at failure when the column can buckle only about the x-axis.

2. Pin-ended columns

The failure criterion for pin-ended columns is based on the nominal maximum stress at the centre of the column:

$$(P_T \Delta / Z_x F_{bu}) + (P_T / A F_{cu}) = 1 \tag{19}$$

where P_T is the maximum applied axial load, Δ is the maximum deflection, Z_x is the section modulus and F_{bu} is the ultimate bending strength.

From equations (6) to (8) in annex I, the deflection Δ is given by

$$\Delta = \Delta_o (1 + \alpha_T) e^{\alpha_D D^\xi} \tag{20}$$

where Δ_o is the initial value of Δ due to crookedness and

$$\alpha_T = 1 / [(P_{cr(x)} / P_T) - 1] \tag{21}$$

$$\alpha_D = 1 / [(P_{cr(x)} / P_D) - 1] \tag{22}$$

where P_D is the dead load component of the axial load.

The following assumption is now made:

$$F_{cu} = 0.75 \, F_{bu} \tag{23}$$

Noting that

$$f_{cxu} = P_T / A \tag{24}$$

then equations (17) to (24) lead to

$$k_{cxu} = 1 / [0.75 \, \Delta_o (A/Z_x)(1 + \alpha_T) e^{\alpha_D D^\xi} + 1] \tag{25}$$

$$\alpha_T = 1 / \{[0.822 (E/F_{cu}) / S_{cx}^2 k_{cxu}] - 1\} \tag{26}$$

$$\alpha_D = 1 / \{[0.822 (E/F_{cu}) / r_c S_{cx}^2 k_{cxu}] - 1\} \tag{27}$$

where

$$r_c = P_D / P_T \tag{28}$$

Since the unknown quantity k_{cxu} appears in the three equations (25) to (27), the solution can be obtained only through iteration.

3. Pin-ended rectangular columns

For the case of rectangular columns,

$$A = bd \tag{29}$$

$$Z_x = bd^2 / 6 \tag{30}$$

where b and d are the breadth and depth, respectively, of the cross-section (figure 32).

Figure 32. Notation for beam-column

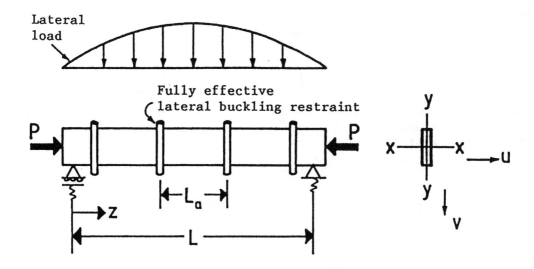

Furthermore, it will be assumed that the initial crookedness is a curvature such that

$$\Delta_o = a_{co}L^2/d \tag{31}$$

where L is the length of the column and a_{co} is a specified dimensionless constant.

The substitution of equations (29) and (30) into equations (17) and (25) leads to

$$S_{cx} = L/d \tag{32}$$

$$k_{cxu} = 1/[4.5\ a_{co}S_{cx}{}^2(1 + \alpha_T)e^{\alpha_D{}^\xi} + 1] \tag{33}$$

where α_T and α_D are defined by equations (26) and (27).

In limited in-grade studies of buckling strength, it was found that the data fitted $4.5\ a_{co} = 0.0004$, which leads to

$$k_{cxu} = 1/[0.0004\ S_{cs}{}^2(1 + \alpha_T)e^{\alpha_D{}^\xi} + 1] \tag{34}$$

D. Beams

1. General

For beams, the use of equations (5) and (23) leads to the slenderness coefficient S_{bx} for a beam bending about the major or x-axis, defined by

$$S_{bx} = (1.1\ EZ_x/M_{cr(x)})^{1/2} \tag{35}$$

where $M_{cr(x)}$ is the elastic buckling moment. The stability factor for the buckling strength, denoted by k_{bxu}, is defined by

$$f_{bxu} = k_{bxu}F_{bu} \tag{36}$$

where f_{bxu} is the nominal applied bending stress at failure.

2. Simply-supported beams

For simple, symmetrically loaded, end-supported beams, the failure criteria will be based on the nominal maximum stress due to the maximum moment M_T at the centre of the beam:

$$(M_T/Z_x F_{bu}) + (M_T/Z_y F_{bu}) = 1 \tag{37}$$

where Z_x and Z_y are section moduli and ϕ is the maximum rotation (about the z-axis) at the centre of the beam (figure 32). From equations (6) to (8) in annex I, the twist ϕ is given by

$$\phi = \phi_o(1 + \alpha_T)e^{\alpha_D \xi} \tag{38}$$

where ϕ_o is the initial value of   due to crookedness and

$$\alpha_T = 1/[(M_{cr(x)}/M_T) - 1] \tag{39}$$

$$\alpha_D = 1/[(M_{cr(x)}/M_D) - 1] \tag{40}$$

where M_D is the dead load component of the applied moment.

Noting that

$$f_{bxu} = M_T/Z_x \tag{41}$$

equations (35) to (41) lead to

$$k_{bxu} = 1/[\phi_o(Z_x/Z_y)(1 + \alpha_T)e^{\alpha_D \xi} + 1] \tag{42}$$

where

$$\alpha_T = 1/\{[0.822 (E/F_{cu})/S_{bx}^2 k_{bxu}] - 1\} \tag{43}$$

$$\alpha_D = 1/\{[0.822 (E/F_{cu})/r_b S_{bx}^2 k_{bxu}] - 1\} \tag{44}$$

where

$$r_b = M_D/M_T \tag{45}$$

The similarity between equations (25) to (27) and (42) to (44) is to be noted.

3. Simply-supported rectangular beams

For the case of rectangular beams,

$$Z_x = bd^2/6 \tag{46a}$$

$$Z_y = b^2d/6 \tag{46b}$$

Furthermore, it will be assumed that a good approximation to the elastic buckling moment is given by the following [3]:

$$M_{cr(x)} = 0.1 Eb^3d/L_a \tag{47}$$

where L_a is the distance between effective lateral restraints.

The initial twist parameter ϕ_0 will be taken to be given by

$$\phi_0 = a_{bo}L_a/b \tag{48}$$

Substitution of equations (46) to (48) into (35) and (42) to (44) leads to

$$S_{bx} = 1.35(L_a d/b^2)^{1/2} \tag{49}$$

$$k_{bxu} = 1/[0.546 \, a_{bo}S_{bx}^2(1 + \alpha_T)e^{\alpha_D \xi} + 1] \tag{50}$$

where α_T and α_D are defined by equations (43) and (44).

In limited in-grade studies of buckling strength, it was found that the data fitted $0.546 \, a_{bo} = 0.0001$, which leads to

$$k_{bxu} = 1/[0.0001 \, S_{bx}^2(1 + \alpha_T)e^{\alpha_D \xi} + 1] \tag{51}$$

The similarity between equations (34) and (51) is to be noted.

E. Design equations

1. Rectangular columns

For rectangular columns with simple pin ends, the equations derived for the ultimate buckling strength are applicable except that the ultimate compression strength F_{cu} is replaced by the allowable design strength F_c and a safety factor of 3 is used on the modulus of elasticity E in order to allow for variations in both modulus and end fixity conditions.

Thus the stability factor for design k_{cx} is defined by

$$f_{cx} = k_{cx}F_c \tag{52}$$

where f_{cx} is the allowable nominal design stress.

The slenderness coefficient is defined by

$$S_{cx} = L/d \tag{53}$$

and the stability factor is given by

$$k_{cx} = 1/[0.0004 \, S_{cx}^2(1 + \alpha_T)e^{\alpha_D \xi} + 1] \tag{54}$$

$$\alpha_T = 1/\left\{[0.274(E/F_c)/S_{cx}^2 k_{cx}] - 1\right\} \tag{55}$$

$$\alpha_D = 1/\left\{[0.274(E/F_c)/r_c S_{cx}^2 k_{cx}] - 1\right\} \tag{56}$$

where

$$r_c = P_D'/P_T' \tag{57}$$

where P_D' and P_T' are the design dead and total loads, respectively.

For the case of buckling about the y-axis, a stability factor k_{cy}, dependent on a slenderness coefficient S_{cy}, may be obtained in a manner analogous to that of k_{cx}.

2. Rectangular beams

The design formulae for simple rectangular beams are derived in the same way as for columns. Thus, the stability factor k_{bx} is defined by

$$f_{bx} = k_{bx}F_b \tag{58}$$

where f_{bx} is the allowable nominal design bending stress and F_b is the design bending strength for stable members.

The slenderness coefficient is defined by

$$S_{bx} = 1.35(L_ad/b^2) \tag{59}$$

and the stability factor is given by

$$k_{bx} = 1/[0.0001\ S_{bx}^2(1 + \alpha_T)e^{\alpha_D\xi} + 1] \tag{60}$$

$$\alpha_T = 1/\left\{[(0.274(E/F_c)/S_{bx}^2k_{bx}] - 1\right\} \tag{61}$$

$$\alpha_D = 1/\left\{[0.274(E/F_c)/r_bS_{bx}^2k_{bx}] - 1\right\} \tag{62}$$

where

$$r_b = M_D'/M_T' \tag{63}$$

in which M_D' and M_T' are the moments due to the design dead and total loads, respectively.

3. General beams and columns

Buckling strength predictions are not highly accurate because this strength is influenced by many factors that are difficult to assess.

Examples of such factors are crookedness, non-linear material characteristics, end fixity conditions and creep mechanics. Because of this, a high degree of refinement in the derivation procedures is not warranted. Accordingly, it is recommended that slenderness coefficients for beams and columns in general be derived according to the following equation, analogous to equation (5):

$$S = [(\pi^2/12)(E/F_c)(F/F_{cr})]^{1/2} \tag{64}$$

where F denotes the allowable design stress permitted for stable members. Then the required stability factors k_{cx} and k_{bx} are taken to be the same as those given by equations (54) and (60), respectively. The buckling stress F_{cr} for many useful practical cases has been given by Bleich [4], Clark and Hill [5], Nethercot and Rockey [6] and Timoshenko and Gere [7].

F. Normalization of design equations

For simplicity in code application, the following further approximations are introduced:

$$a_{co} \cong (a_{co}/1000)(E/F_c) \tag{65}$$

$$a_{bo} \cong (a_{bo}/1000)(E/F_c) \tag{66}$$

Equations (65) and (66) are obviously exact for the typical case $E/F_c = 1000$. Substitution of these equations into equations (54) to (56) leads to the following stability factor for columns:

$$k_{cs} = 1/[0.4\ S_{cxo}^2(1 + \alpha_T)e^{\alpha_D \xi} + 1] \tag{67}$$

$$\alpha_T = 1/[(0.274/S_{cxo}^2 k_{cx}) - 1] \tag{68}$$

$$\alpha_D = 1/[(0.274/r_c S_{cxo}^2 k_{cx}) - 1] \tag{69}$$

where

$$S_{cxo} = S_{cx}(F_c/E)^{1/2} \tag{70}$$

Similarly, substitution of these equations into (60) to (62) leads to the following stability factor for beams:

$$k_{bx} = 1/[0.1\ S_{bxo}^2(1 + \alpha_T)e^{\alpha_D \xi} + 1] \tag{71}$$

$$\alpha_T = 1/[(0.274/S_{bxo}^2 k_{bx}) - 1] \tag{72}$$

$$\alpha_D = 1/[(0.274/r_b S_{bxo}^2 k_{bx}) - 1] \tag{73}$$

where

$$S_{bxo} = S_{bx}(F_c/E)^{1/2} \tag{74}$$

Equations (67) to (69) and (71) to (73) are normalized and enable the stability factors to be tabulated independently of material properties. These stability factors are plotted in figure 33.

Figure 33.   Examples of stability factors

Stability factor k

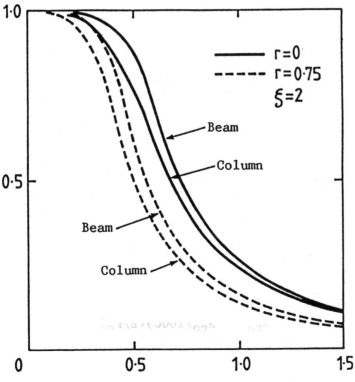

Slenderness coefficient $S\sqrt{F_c/E}$

As noted earlier, equations (67) to (74) do not have a closed form solution and hence are not suitable for direct application in design codes. For this case, a useful good approximation is given by

$$k = 1/[1 + (2 + 0.25 \xi r)^{2\beta} S^{2\beta}]^{1/\beta} \tag{75}$$

where $\beta = 2.5$ for columns and $\beta = 3.0$ for beams. In equation (75), depending on whether a column or beam is referred to, the notation k is used to denote either k_{cx} or k_{bx}, the notation r is used to denote either r_c or r_b and the notation S is used to denote either S_{cxo} or S_{bxo}.

G. Interaction equations

Many practical structural elements, such as the top chord of a truss, are susceptible to buckling simultaneously in several ways or to combined buckling and other stresses. Annex II gives a theoretical analysis of a beam-column member subjected to combined bending and axial forces. The resultant equations are too complex for practical application and, for the reasons mentioned in the previous section, are of dubious accuracy. Hence, the use of simple interaction equations, fitted to the analytical solutions or to any available experimental data, appears appropriate.

For the case of combined bending about the x-axis and axial compression, the following interaction formula may be used:

$$(f_{bx}/k_{bx}F_b) + (f_c/F_c)^{2/\eta}[(1/k_{cx})^2 + (1/k_{cy})^2 = 1]^{1/\eta} \leqq 1 \tag{76}$$

A value of $\eta = 4$ in equation (76) provides a reasonable fit with the analytical solution derived in annex II. However, because that analysis contains many conservative assumptions, a more realistic recommendation is probably to use the value $\eta = 2$.

For the case of combined bending and tension, the following interaction formulae may be used:

$$(f_b/F_b) + (f_t/F_t) \leqq 1 \tag{77a}$$

$$(f_b - f_t)/(k_{bx}F_b) \leqq 1 \tag{77b}$$

Both equations must be satisfied. Equation (77a) is intended to take account of the situation when the tension edge is critical, and equation (77b) when the buckling strength is critical.

It should be mentioned that in the application of equation (77a), the applied bending moment may be reduced because of the negative bending moment applied by the axial load. This reduction may be taken conservatively as $0.6T\Delta$, where T is the axial tension force and Δ is the theoretical deflection due to the lateral load acting alone.

H. Buckling restraints

1. General procedure

Buckling restraints are frequently introduced to increase the allowable working load on slender members. They are also often present as part of a secondary structural system. Normally these restraints are considered to act as effectively rigid restraints and are designed with the use of semi-empirical rules. However, for important structures a more careful assessment of the performance of buckling restraints must be made. Two important design aspects of buckling restraints are their effect on the strength of the primary structure and their capacity to carry the loads placed on them by the primary structure.

The theoretical analysis of buckling restraint systems is quite complex, and because of the uncertainties of input information, exact analyses are not warranted. A suitable approximate method has been examined elsewhere [8] and will be described herein.

The first part of the analysis is to estimate the design strength of the member when stabilized by a restraint system. For this, it is necessary to include the effect of the restraint system in evaluating the slenderness coefficient of the member according to equation (64). It is sufficiently accurate to guess at a reasonable buckling mode shape and to use it in the energy method of analysis [7] to derive an approximate buckling load λ_{cr}. With the slenderness coefficient so derived, a stability factor k_c or k_b is computed as for a beam or column and an allowable design load λ_a is obtained.

To compute the force acting on the restraint system, a pseudo buckling load λ_{cro} is first derived in the same way as λ_{cr}, except that the assumed buckling mode shape is taken to be that of the initial deformation due to crookedness of the unloaded member.

Then, the elastic displacement Δ_e at a restraint point is taken to be given by

$$\Delta_e = \Delta_o/[(\lambda_{cro}/\lambda_a) - 1] \qquad (78)$$

where Δ_o is the initial displacement of the unloaded member. The load on the restraint system due to this displacement is $K_R\Delta_e$, where K_R is the stiffness of the restraint.

For long-duration loads, an allowance must be made for the fact that creep will effectively increase the value of Δ_o.

Details of methods for adopting such analytical solutions for use in design codes have been given elsewhere [9].

2. Example

For a pin-ended column, such as that shown in figure 34, strengthened by N equally spaced lateral restraints, each with stiffness K_R, the variational strain energy δV is given by

$$\delta V = 1/2 \sum_{t=1}^{N} K_R u_t + 1/2\int_{o}^{L} [EI(d^2u/dz^2)^2 - P_{cr}(du/dz)^2]dz \qquad (79)$$

Figure 34.   Notation for column with lateral restraints

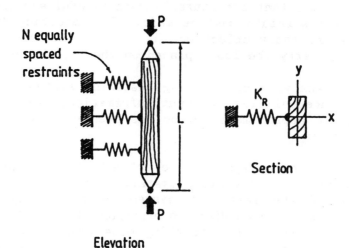

If it is assumed that the buckling mode shape is given by

$$u = a \sin(n\pi 2/L) \tag{80}$$

then the equation $\delta V = 0$ leads to

$$P_{cr}(n) = n^2 P_0, \text{ if } n = N + 1 \tag{81a}$$

$$Pcr(n) = Po[n2 + (\Omega/n2)], \text{ if } n \neq N + 1 \tag{81b}$$

where

$$P_0 = \pi^2 E I_y/L^2 \tag{82}$$

$$\Omega = (N + 1) K_R L/(\pi^2 P_0) \tag{83}$$

The appropriate value of n to be used in equation (81) is the value that leads to the smallest value of P_{cr}.   A conservative approximation to equation (81b) is given by the condition $\partial P_{cr}/\partial n = 0$, which leads to

$$P_{cr} = P_0 [4\Omega]^{1/2} \tag{84}$$

Equations (81) and (84) are illustrated in figure 35 for the case N = 2.

From equations (81a) and (84) it can be seen that equation (84) is valid for the range $\Omega \leq 0.25(N + 1)^4$. For the range $\Omega \leq 0.25(N + 1)$, the elastic buckling load is given by

$$P_{cr} = (N + 1)^2 P_0 \tag{85}$$

Hence from equations (64), (84) and (85), the slenderness coefficient of a laterally restrained rectangular column is given by

$$S_{cy} = (L/b)(4\Omega)^{0.25} \tag{86a}$$

for $\Omega \leq 0.25(N + 1)^4$, and

$$S_{cy} = (L/b)/(N + 1) \tag{86b}$$

for $\Omega \geq 0.25(N + 1)^4$. Equation (86a) represents the practical range of restraint stiffness.

Figure 35. Effect of restraint stiffness on buckling load

Buckling load P_{cr}/P_o

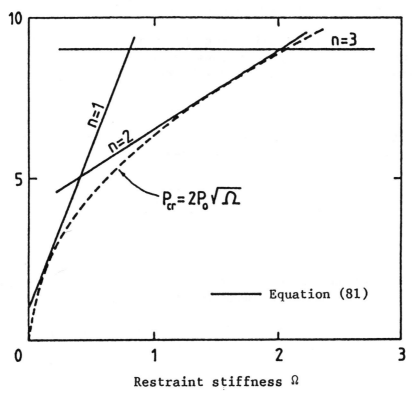

Restraint stiffness Ω

To compute the force in the lateral restraint, it is reasonable to assume that the initial crookedness u_o has the form

$$u_o = a_o \sin(\mu z/L) \tag{87}$$

Hence from equations (78), (81) and (87) the force P_R on a restraint located near the centre of the column is given by

$$P_R = a_o K_R/[(P_{cr(1)}/P) - 1] \tag{88}$$

where $P_{cr(1)}$ is given by

$$P_{cr(1)} = P_o(1 + \Omega) \tag{89}$$

Annex I

CREEP DEFORMATIONS OF SLENDER BEAMS AND COLUMNS

The initial crookedness and deformations under load of a beam or column may be described in terms of eigenmode shapes [10]. Although it is a simple matter to include all the eigenmode shapes in the analysis, the meagre data available on crookedness do not justify consideration of more than the primary eigenmode, the mode corresponding to the lowest elastic buckling load.

Since elastic, buckling and creep deformations are all in the primary eigenmode shape, it is necessary to consider only the lateral deflection Δ of an arbitrary point. This deflection may be written

$$\Delta = \Delta_s + \Delta_e \tag{1}$$

where Δ_s is the lateral deflection that would remain if the member were unloaded. The elastic deflection Δ_e is given by

$$\Delta_e = \alpha \Delta_s \tag{2}$$

where

$$\alpha = 1/[(\lambda_{cr}/\lambda) - 1] \tag{3}$$

where λ is the load parameter and λ_{cr} is the elastic buckling value of λ corresponding to the primary eigenmode shape.

Since deflections are proportional to the strains, the constitutive equation (13) in the main text may be written

$$d\Delta_s/dm = - \Delta_e h(m) \tag{4}$$

Substituting equation (2) into (4) and integrating with respect to Δ_s and m shows that for a member allowed to creep under dead load λ_D, the permanent set Δ_s is given by

$$\Delta_s = \Delta_o e^{\alpha_D \xi} \tag{5}$$

where ξ is the creep factor defined by equation (15) in the main text and α_D is the amplification factor given by

$$\alpha_D = 1/[(\lambda_{cr}/\lambda_D) - 1] \tag{6}$$

If at the end of the creep period the applied load parameter is increased to λ_T, then equations (1), (2) and (5) lead to the deflection Δ, given by

$$\Delta = \Delta_0 (1 + \alpha_T) e^{\alpha_D \xi} \tag{7}$$

where

$$\alpha_T = 1/[(\lambda_{cr}/\lambda_T) - 1] \tag{8}$$

Annex II

BUCKLING STRENGTH OF BEAM-COLUMNS

A. Deformations

The beam-column under consideration is shown in figure 32. Apart from an axial load P, a lateral load is applied in the y direction, bending the beam about the major or x-axis. It is the purpose of section A of this annex to estimate the deformations in the y-direction. In section B, the effects of the lateral deformations will also be considered.

The total deflection in the y-direction, denoted by v, will be taken to be given by

$$v = v_s + v_b + v_c \tag{1}$$

where v_s is the deformation that would remain if the beam-column were unloaded, v_b is the deflection due to the lateral load acting alone and v_c is the additional deflection obtained on applying the axial load P. For simplicity, it will be assumed that the beam-column is simply supported and that the deflections are all sine waves as follows:

$$v = \Delta \sin(\pi z/L) \tag{2}$$

$$v_s = \Delta_s \sin(\pi z/L) \tag{3}$$

$$v_b = \Delta_b \sin(\pi z/L) \tag{4}$$

$$v_c = \Delta_c \sin(\pi z/L) \tag{5}$$

Equations (1) to (5) show that the central deflection Δ may be written

$$\Delta = \Delta_s + \Delta_b + \Delta_c \tag{6}$$

From equation (4), the applied bending moment M_a is

$$M_a = M_o \sin(\pi z/L) \tag{7}$$

where

$$M_o = (\pi/L)^2 EI_x \Delta_b \tag{8}$$

For the case of a simple pin-ended column,

$$P_{cr(x)} = \pi^2 EI_x/L^2 \tag{9}$$

and so equation (8) may be written

$$\Delta_b = M_o/P_{cr(x)} \tag{10}$$

The actual total bending moment at the centre of the beam-column is

$$M_{max} = M_o + P\Delta \tag{11}$$

It is also given by

$$M_{max} = (\pi/L)^2 EI_x(\Delta_b + \Delta_c) \tag{12}$$

Equations (6) to (12) lead to

$$\Delta_c = \alpha(\Delta_s + \Delta_b) \tag{13}$$

where

$$\alpha = 1/[(P_{cr(x)}/P) - 1] \tag{14}$$

Hence the total deflection Δ is given by

$$\Delta = (1 + \alpha)(\Delta_s + \Delta_b) \tag{15}$$

Since all deformations are sine shapes, displacements are proportional to the strains, and equation (13) in the main text may be written

$$d\Delta_s/dm = - (\Delta_b + \Delta_c)h(m) \tag{16}$$

From equations (13) and (16),

$$d\Delta_s/dm = - [(1 + \alpha)\Delta_b + \alpha\Delta_s]h(m) \tag{17}$$

Integrating equation (17) leads to

$$\Delta_s = \Delta_o e^{\alpha D\xi} + \Delta_b[1 + (1/\alpha)](e^{\alpha\xi} - 1) \tag{18}$$

where Δ_o is the initial value of the crookedness Δ_s and ξ is the creep factor defined by equation (15) in the main text.

If it is assumed that the beam-column creeps under the influence of the dead loads $P = P_D$ and $M_o = M_D$ and that the loads are later increased by the addition of live loads to $P = P_T$ and $M_o = M_T$, then equations (14), (15) and (18) lead to the maximum deflection Δ given by

$$\Delta = \Delta_o \left((1 + \alpha_T)e^{\alpha D\xi} + (M_T/P_T)\alpha_T + r_b\alpha_T[1 + (1/\alpha_D)](e^{\alpha D\xi} - 1) \right) \tag{19}$$

where

$$\alpha_T = 1/[(P_{cr(x)}/P_T) - 1] \tag{20}$$

$$\alpha_D = 1/[(P_{cr(x)}/P_D) - 1] \tag{21}$$

$$r_b = M_D/M_T \tag{22}$$

B. Strength

The beam-column shown in figure 32 can deflect in both the x and y directions and it can twist. Hence, the failure criterion will be taken to be given by

$$[(M_T + \Delta P_T)/Z_x k_{bxu}F_{bu}] + (P_T/Ak_{cyu}F_{cu}) = 1 \tag{23}$$

Equation (23) is similar to the failure criteria stated in equations (19) and (37) in the main text for the case of stable members but tends to be conservative as the members become slender [4].

Noting that equations (18) to (20) in the main text lead to

$$\Delta_o(1 + \alpha_T)e^{\alpha D\xi} = (Z_x F_{bu}/A)[(1/f_{cxu}) - (1/F_{cu})]$$

and using the following definitions

$$f_{cu} = P_T/A$$

$$f_{bu} = M_T/Z_x$$

equations (19) and (22) lead to

$$\phi(f_{bu}/k_{bxu}F_{bu}) + (1/k_{bxu})[(f_{cu}/k_{cxu}F_{cu}) - (f_{cu}/F_{cu})] + (f_{cu}/k_{cyu}F_{cu}) = 1 \quad (24)$$

where

$$\phi = 1 + \alpha_T + r_b\alpha_T[1 + (1/\alpha_D)][e^{\alpha_D^\xi} - 1] \quad (25)$$

Equation (24) is an interaction equation for the failure criterion under the combined nominal applies stresses f_{cu} and f_{bu}.

References

1. R. H. Leicester, "A rheological model for mechano-sorptive deflections of beams", Wood Science and Technology, vol. 5, No. 3 (1971), pp. 211-220.

2. R. H. Leicester, "Lateral deflections of timber beam-columns during drying", Wood Science and Technology, vol. 5, No. 3 (1971), pp. 221-231.

3. R. F. Hooley and B. Madsen, "Lateral stability of glued laminated beams", American Society of Civil Engineers: Structural Division: Journal, vol. 90, No. ST3 (June 1964).

4. F. Bleich, Buckling Strength of Metal Structures (New York, McGraw Hill, 1952).

5. J. W. Clark and H. N. Hill, "Lateral buckling of beams", American Society of Civil Engineers: Structural Division: Journal, vol. 86, No. ST7 (July 1960), pp. 175-195.

6. D. A. Nethercot and K. C. Rockey, "A unified approach to the elastic lateral buckling of beams", Structural Engineer, vol. 49, No. 7 (July 1971), pp. 321-330. (For Erratum see vol. 51, No. 4 (April 1973), pp. 138-139.)

7. S. P. Timoshenko and J. M. Gere, Theory of Elastic Stability, 2nd ed. (New York, McGraw Hill, 1961).

8. R. H. Leicester, "Design of structural systems with restraints against buckling", Proceedings of Conference on Metal Structures and the Practicing Engineer (Melbourne, Institution of Engineers, November 1974), pp. 23-26.

9. R. H. Leicester, "Design of bracing systems for timber structures", Proceedings of 17th Forest Products Research Conference (Melbourne, CSIRO, Division of Chemical and Wood Technology, May 1975).

10. R. H. Leicester, "Southwell plot for beam-columns", American Society of Civil Engineers: Engineering Mechanics Division: Journal, vol. 96, No. EM6 (December 1970), pp. 945-965.

IV. DERIVATION OF DESIGN PROPERTIES

Robert H. Leicester*

A. Evaluation procedures

One of the fundamental difficulties associated with the drafting of timber engineering design codes and the associated specification standards is that until recently there were no standards related to the performance requirements of structural timber elements in general or stress-graded timber in particular. Design values for structural timber elements have been derived essentially through lengthy periods of trial and error. A summary of the methods traditionally used in Australia is given in the annex.

The trial and error procedure is unsatisfactory for many reasons. It is too slow for practical purposes when new evaluation techniques arise or new types of structural elements are introduced; also, it does not provide a rational basis for modifying existing methods when changes occur in technological, economic or social conditions. Thus, research aimed at optimizing the structural utilization of timber cannot be placed within a national framework, and it becomes difficult to resolve commercial conflicts between competing structural elements and grading systems.

A further frustrating aspect of the above is the difficulty of taking advantage of new research information. For example, one traditional method for the derivation of the basic design bending stress, to be denoted B^O, is the following:

$$B^O = B^C_{0.01} GF/(1.75 \times 1.25) \tag{1}$$

where $B^C_{0.01}$ denotes the one-percentile value of the small clear bending strength; GF denotes the grade factor, which is taken to be the average reduction in strength owing to the presence of the maximum permissible defect; the 1.75 factor is the effect of a long duration load; and the 1.25 factor is a contingency factor. Problems arise when a grader requests permission to omit the 1.25 factor because he is more careful than the average grader, when research indicates that the coefficient of variation of clear material differs from that of structurally graded material or when the grade factor GF and/or the duration of load factor 1.75 are incorrect. Since there are many other uncertainties associated with design, it is not readily apparent whether equation (1), derived through many years of practical application, does in fact still lead to an optimum design value, or whether a change is in order in the light of new research information.

During the past decade the situation has improved in that there is now an implicit acceptance by many countries to use the five-percentile strength of graded material as a characteristic value; the design strength is then taken to be proportional to this value. The extensive evaluation studies by Madsen, the Forest Products Laboratory at Vancouver and the Princes Risborough Laboratory have been directed towards determination of this characeristic value [1], [2], [3], [4], [5], [6].

*An officer of CSIRO, Division of Building Research, Melbourne.

In recent years, a strong incentive for the rational derivation of design properties has arisen due to the fact that in many countries, including Australia, and in many international standards organizations, such as the International Organization for Standardization and the Eurocode group of the European Community, the principle has been accepted that the procedure to be used for the derivation of the safety level in all structural codes, both for materials and loads, will be under the control of a single coordinating committee. In its simplest form, the format to be used to derive a design stress R* is either

$$R^* = \phi R_{0.05} \qquad (2a)$$

or

$$R^* = R_{0.05}/\gamma \qquad (2b)$$

where $R_{0.05}$ is the five-percentile characteristic strength value of the structural member in service, ϕ is a material factor and γ is a load factor or design coefficient. The material factor ϕ and the load factor γ depend on the statistical characeristics of the strength R, illustrated in figure 36.

Figure 36. Characteristic strength $R_{0.05}$

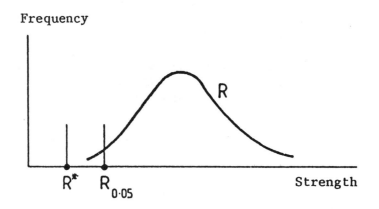

The characteristic value chosen for stiffness properties, such as the modulus of elasticity, is usually taken to be the five-percentile value when used to compute the buckling strength of slender members and the mean value when used to compute deflections.

A significant feature of this latest development is that the structural element is now to be treated as a "black box". The material factors to be used do not depend on knowing the composition of the element; the factors are now stated as a function only of the intended end use and the statistical characteristics of the structural properties of the element. This is obviously a change from the traditional procedures in which the specified material factors, such as those given for connectors in the annex, are determined to a large extent by the composition of the structural element.

An important implication of the above is that structural timber elements will have to be designed so that they show the same structural reliability as elements of other structural materials, such as steel and reinforced concrete, when they are intended to be used for the same end use.

B. Safety index

Current reliability methods for the derivation of load factors are related to the concept of a safety index. In formal terms, this safety index, usually denoted by the term β, is defined by

$$\Phi(-\beta) = p_F \tag{3}$$

where p_F is the probability of failure associated with a structural design and $\Phi()$ is the cumulative frequency distribution of a unit normal variate. Equation (3) is tabulated in table 7. A good approximation to equation (3) for the practical range $2.5 < \beta < 5.0$ is given by

$$\beta = 1.2 - 0.6 \log_{10}(p_F) \tag{4}$$

Table 7. Safety index β defined by equation (3)

p_F	β
10^{-2}	2.33
10^{-3}	3.09
10^{-4}	3.72
10^{-5}	4.26
10^{-6}	4.75
10^{-8}	5.61

Equations (3) and (4) are shown in figure 37.

Figure 37. Relationship between the safety index and the probability of failure

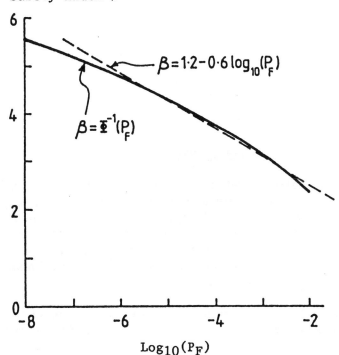

Safety index

To illustrate the application of equation (3), it will be applied to the simple case where the load effects S and strength R can be represented by two lognormal random variables as shown in figure 38. For this case, it can be shown that β is given by

$$\beta \cong \log_e(\bar{R}/\bar{S})/(V_R^2 + V_S^2)^{0.5} \tag{5}$$

This can be written

$$\bar{R}/\bar{S} = \exp[\beta(V_R^2 + V_S^2)^{0.5}] \cong \exp[0.75\beta(V_R + V_S)] \tag{6}$$

where $\bar{R}$ and $\bar{S}$ are the mean values of R and S and V_R and V_S are the corresponding coefficients of variation.

Figure 38. Statistical distribution of load effect and strength

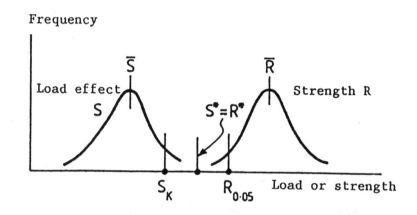

Equation (6) may be written in the form of the design criterion

$$R* = S* \tag{7}$$

where the design strength R* and load effect S* are given by

$$R* = \bar{R}\exp(-0.75\ \beta V_R) \tag{8}$$

$$S* = \bar{S}\exp(0.75\ \beta V_S) \tag{9}$$

Equations (2) and (8) lead to the material factor

$$\phi = (\bar{R}/R_{0.05})\exp(-0.75\ \beta V_R) \tag{10}$$

The appropriate safety index β is decided by a coordinating structural engineering committee. The recommended value of β is usually chosen to match that obtained in typical current designs; this procedure is referred to as a calibration. The values that have been obtained from existing design codes tend to vary from country to country and from one material to another. Some typical values for building components are as follows: beams and columns, $\beta = 2.5-4.5$ and connectors, $\beta = 4.0-6.0$.

A rational derivation of the safety index β can be obtained from optimized reliability considerations in which the cost of failure relative to the cost

cost of a structural element is considered. Obviously, such an approach would lead to a greater safety index for connectors than for beams. This is in accordance with the empirical values shown above.

For most countries, including Australia, a procedure more complex than the simple application of equation (10) is used to evaluate the design coefficient ϕ. The method involves the computation of the probability of failure for structural members subjected to combinations of loads, including loads that fluctuate with time, such as wind loads and floor live loads. The algorithm used for computing the probability of failure is quite straightforward, but the calibration procedure can be difficult because of the poor availability of the required statistical information.

It is outside the scope of this chapter to discuss the matter of material factors in detail. Figure 39 shows a set of graphs derived from a calibration procedure with Australian design codes. It may be used to obtain a reasonably good estimate of material factors for specified strengths in Australian structural design codes.

Figure 39. Material factors for various target safety indices

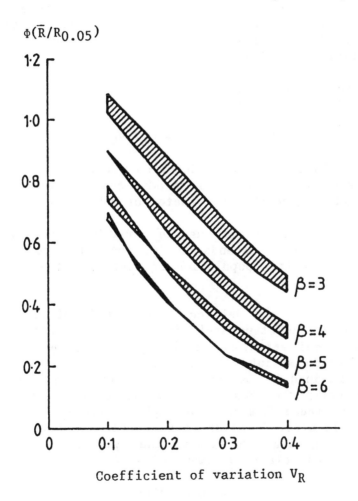

C. Material factors for Australian standards

1. Graded timber

The current Australian recommendations for evaluating the design properties of graded timber are given in the draft standard that is annexed to the
chapter "Structural grading of timber", contained in the volume Structural
Timber and Related Products (ID/SER.0/7). Specifically, test methods for evaluating the bending, tension, compression and shear strengths and also the
modulus of elasticity are mentioned. Some matters of interest in this standard are the following:

(a) The design properties are related to a specific reference population;

(b) The five-percentile value is chosen as the characteristic value;

(c) For sample sizes of less than 400, the reduction factor
$(1 - 3 V_R/\sqrt{N})$ is used to provide the required reliability on the characteristic values. Here N denotes the sample size and V_R denotes the coefficient
of variation in the strength property;

(d) For each design property, a standard configuration for method of
loading and specimen size is given. In particular, a random location of
defects is specified. Where standard test conditions are not obtained, an
appropriate modification factor is given;

(e) The load factor γ recommended for the derivation of basic working
stresses is taken to be given by

$$\gamma = 1.75(1.3 + 0.7 \, V_R) \tag{11}$$

where the factor 1.75 is a nominal duration factor to convert 5-min strength
to the basic working stress, which is traditionally taken to be that relevant
to a permanent load. Hence the true factor of safety is $(1.3 + 0.7 \, V_R)$.

It is important to note that use of equation (11) indicates that since
the appropriate load factor depends on V_R, then the design stress is a property assigned to a specific population of timber. It is not the property of
a single stick.

When design stresses are derived on the basis of information other than
that from tests on graded structural timber, implicit use is made of information obtained on graded structural timber of other species. Thus additional
uncertainty is introduced into the estimate of structural properties. This
matter has been examined by Leicester and Hawkins [7], who estimate that if
load factors are correctly chosen to give a specified reliability, then the
design stresses of graded timber of any given species that have been derived
on the basis of full-size, in-grade tests should be about 25 per cent greater
than the corresponding values for timber that has been evaluated solely on the
basis of tests on small, clear specimens of wood.

2. Connectors

AS 1649 [8] provides a suitable basis for evaluating the design properties of metal connectors. However, the load factors specified in the current
code have not been chosen to fit existing design recommendations for specific
fasteners. As a result, it is not clear whether the strength or deformation

requirements are the necessary ones, or even whether the load factors specified are optimum values.

3. Other structural elements

For structural elements other than solid timber, such as plywood and
glulam, there are no existing Australian recommendations that are based on
reliability considerations. However, there is no reason why the procedures
proposed for graded timber cannot be adopted here.

4. System effects

The above discussion has concerned the structural reliability of single
elements. When multiple-element structures such as floor and roof truss systems are used, the reliabilities of the elements interact to produce system
effects. Some system effects, such as the weakest link effect, can reduce the
nominal safety, while other system effects, such as the load-sharing effect,
can increase it.

A typical example of a weakest link effect would be a single isolated
truss for which the failure of a single element, either timber or connector,
would be catastrophic to both the truss and the building structure. If the
system contains N similar elements, each with a coefficient of variation V_R
and with all strengths being uncorrelated, then it can be shown that the
characteristic value of the system $R_{0.05(sys)}$ relative to that of a single
member $R_{0.05}$ is given roughly by

$$R_{0.05(sys)} = R_{0.05}/N^{V_R} \tag{12}$$

The load-sharing effect of parallel systems is illustrated in figures 40
and 41. Where several similar elements deform together, as is indicated in
figure 40, the average normalized strength tends to be greater than that of
the weakest member when this member is exceptionally weak. Thus, the characteristic value of the system is increased, as indicated in figure 41. Load-
sharing factors obtained in this way for both beam and grid systems have been
studied by Leicester and Reardon [9] for several Australian structural timbers. For example, the load-sharing factor related to the five-percentile
characteristic strength of five beams deflecting together, as may occur in
vertically nailed laminated construction, were found to be the following:

Timber	Load-sharing factor
Slash pine (pith-in)	1.22
Radiata pine (F5)	1.19
Messmate (F14)	1.11

The results of these studies have been considered in deriving the load-sharing
factors for AS 1720 [10].

Figure 40. Method for evaluating the load deformation
characteristics of a parallel system

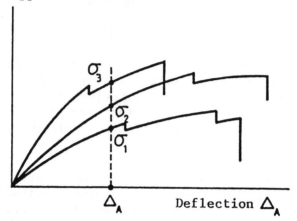

At deflection Δ_A

$$\sigma_{SYS} = \frac{\sigma_1 + \sigma_2 + \sigma_3}{3}$$

Figure 41. Definition of the load-sharing factor for a system

Load-sharing factor = σ_B / σ_A

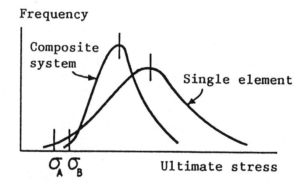

Annex

MATERIAL FACTORS FOR AUSTRALIAN STANDARDS

The information in this annex is taken from a report by Leicester and Keating [11]. The design values are stated in terms of a load factor γ, which is the inverse of the material factor ϕ as indicated by equations (2a) and (2b) in the main text.

Load factors cannot be considered in isolation from other factors, such as the duration of load effects, specified in design standards. Consequently, some care must be exercised in comparing the load factors used in various countries. In Australia, the basic design values of structural properties are obtained by applying load factors to the characteristic values obtained in short-term laboratory tests that last roughly 5 min. The following equation describes the relationship between these three quantities:

Basic design value = Characteristic value/Load factor

In Australian design standards it is stated that the design strengths for a 5 min load duration are to be obtained by multiplying the basic design strength by a factor of 1.75. Hence, the true factors of safety implied in the Australian codes are 1/1.75 = 0.57 times the nominal values of the load factors given in the following sections.

A. Visually graded timber

For timber assessed through tests on small, clear specimens [12] the appropriate load factors used are given in table 8.

Table 8. Characteristic structural properties and load factors for structural lumber assessed from tests on small, clear specimens

Design property for structural lumber	Characteristic value measured on small, clear specimens a/	Load factor b/
Tension strength	One-percentile of F_b'	3.17/GF
Bending strength	One-percentile of F_b'	2.22/GF
Compression strength parallel to grain	One-percentile of F_c'	1.67/GF
Compression strength	Mean limit of proportionality in compression perpendicular to the grain test	1.33
Shear strength of beams	Mean F_v'	4.2/GF
Shear strength of joint details	Mean F_v'	4.7
Modulus of elasticity	Mean	$(0.75/GF)^{0.5}$

a/ F_b', F_c' and F_v' are ultimate strengths in bending, compression and shear in tests on small, clear specimens.

b/ GF = grade factor = the bending strength of structural scantling containing maximum permissible defect divided by the bending strength of a small, clear specimen cut from scantling. The following are typical grade factors used for sawn timber in Australian grading rules: structural grade No. 1, 0.75; structural grade No. 2, 0.60; structural grade No. 3, 0.48; structural grade No. 4, 0.38.

B. In-grade tests on structural lumber

This refers to tests on a specific grade of timber comprising a particular species or mixture of species. Each stick is tested at the worst defect and, in the case of bending tests, with that defect on the tension edge. The basic design stresses in bending B* and tension T* are given by

$$B* = B_{0.05} \times 1.15/1.75(1.2 + 1.4 \; V_B)$$

$$T* = T_{0.05}/1.75(1.2 + 1.4 \; V_T)$$

where $B_{0.05}$ and $T_{0.05}$ denote the five-percentile strength values and V_B and V_T are the coefficients of variation of the measured bending and tension strengths, respectively. If tests are made only on a single population of timber for a particular species, then a contingency factor of 0.9 on B* and T* is used to allow for the occurrence of possible regional effects. The basis of this load factor has been described by Leicester [13].

C. Mechanically stress-graded lumber

The basic design stress in bending is given by

$$B* = B_{0.05}/2.35$$

The basis of this load factor is a personal communication by A. Anton.

D. Pole timbers

Load factors for pole timbers assessed from mechanical tests on small, clear specimens are taken to be the same as those for structural lumber as given in table 8 with an effective grade factor of 0.94. No form factor relative to the use of a round section is to be used in design computations.

E. Plywood

Load factors for plywood assessed from mechanical tests on small, clear specimens are taken to be roughly the same as those for structural timber as given in table 8, with the addition that the load factor for in-plane shear is taken to be 6.4 on the shear-block strength. Associated factors to account for the geometry of the plywood lay-up are given in AS 1720-1975 [10].

F. Metal connectors

The load factors specified in AS 1649-1974 [8] are given in table 9. It is intended that these factors be applied to derive the basic design loads for a particular fastener used with a particular species of timber.

Table 9. Characteristic strength and material coefficients for metal
fasteners assessed from short-duration laboratory tests a/

Type of load	Type of fastener	Characteristic value b/	Load factor
All	All	Mean ultimate strength of fastener metal	2.0
All	All	Mean yield of fastener metal	1.67
Withdrawal	Nails	One-percentile of maximum loads	2.0
Withdrawal	Screws	One-percentile of maximum loads	2.5
Lateral	Nails, screws, staples	One-percentile of maximum loads	4.15
		One-percentile of loads at slip of 0.4 mm	1.25
Lateral	Split rings	One-percentile of maximum loads	2.8
		Average of maximum loads	4.0
Lateral	Toothed plate	One-percentile of maximum loads	2.5
		One-percentile of loads at slip of 0.8 mm	1.6
Lateral	Nailed plate	One-percentile of maximum loads	4.3
		One-percentile of loads at slip of 0.8 mm	1.6

a/ Where two sets of characteristic values and material coefficients are cited, the set to be used is that leading to the smaller design working load.

b/ Slip refers to displacement between the members connected.

References

1. B. Madsen, "Strength values for wood and limit states design", Canadian Journal of Civil Engineering, vol. 2, No. 3 (1975), pp. 270-279.

2. W. M. McGowan, B. Rovner and T. W. Littleford, "Parallel-to-grain tensile properties of dimension lumber from several western Canadian species", Information Report VP-X-172 (Vancouver, Canada, Western Forest Products Laboratory, October 1977).

3. T. W. Littleford, "Flexural properties of dimension lumber for western Canada", Information Report VP-X-179 (Vancouver, Canada, Western Forest Products Laboratory, July 1978).

4. T. W. Littleford and R. A. Abbott, "Parallel-to-grain compressive properties of dimension lumber from western Canada", Information Report VP-X-180 (Vancouver, Canada, Western Forest Products Laboratory, August 1978).

5. W. T. Curry and J. R. Tory, "The relation between modulus of rupture (ultimate bending stress) and modulus of elasticity of timber", Current Paper 30/76 (Princes Risborough, Buckinghamshire, United Kingdom, Princes Risborough Laboratory, Building Research Establishment, April 1976).

6. W. T. Curry and A. R. Fewell, "The relations between the ultimate tension and ultimate compression strength of timber and its modulus of elasticity" (Princes Risborough, Buckinghamshire, United Kingdom, Princes Risborough Laboratory, Building Research Establishment, May 1977).

7. R. H. Leicester and B. T. Hawkins, "Models for evaluating stress grading", 20th Forest Products Conference (Melbourne, CSIRO, Division of Chemical and Wood Technology, 1981).

8. Standards Association of Australia, <u>Australian Standard 1649-1974: Determination of Basic Working Loads for Metal Fasteners for Timber</u> (Sydney, 1974).

9. R. H. Leicester and G. F. Reardon, "Load sharing characteristics of timber structural systems", <u>Proceedings of Conference on Applications of Probability Theory to Structural Design</u> (Melbourne, Institution of Engineers, November 1974), pp. 130-137.

10. Standards Association of Australia, <u>Australian Standard 1720-1975: SAA Timber Engineering Code</u> (Sydney, 1975).

11. R. H. Leicester and W. G. Keating, "Use of strength classifications for timber engineering standards", Technical Paper (Second Series) No. 4 (Melbourne, CSIRO, Division of Building Research, 1982).

12. J. J. Mack, "Australian methods for mechanically testing small clear specimens of timber", Technical Paper (Second Series) No. 31 (Melbourne, CSIRO, Division of Building Research, 1979).

13. R. H. Leicester, "In-grade properties of some Australian timbers", Paper 2/15, 19th Forest Products Research Conference (Melbourne, CSIRO, Division of Chemical and Wood Technology, 1979).

Bibliography

Doyle, D. V. <u>and</u> L. J. Markwardt. Properties of Southern pine in relation to strength grading of dimension lumber. Research paper FPL 64. Madison, Wisconsin, United States Department of Agriculture, Forest Products Laboratory, July 1966.

_____ Tension parallel-to-grain properties of Southern pine dimension lumber. Research paper FPL 84. Madison, Wisconsin, United States Department of Agriculture, Forest Products Laboratory, December 1967.

Madsen, B. In-grade testing, problem analysis. <u>Forest products journal</u> (Madison, Wisconsin) 28:4:42-50, 1978.

Standards Association of Australia. Rules for evaluation of graded timber. Draft standard. Sydney, 1983.

V. EXAMPLES OF THE USE OF AUSTRALIAN STANDARD 1720-1975 TIMBER ENGINEERING CODE, STANDARDS ASSOCIATION OF AUSTRALIA

Robert H. Leicester*

In this chapter, 16 problems are formulated and then solved by applying information contained in AS 1720-1975, on pp. 8 and 9 of which the notation used in setting up and solving the problems here is to be found. The various modification factors K are found on the following pages of the Code:

Modification factor	Page of Code	Modification factor	Page of Code
K_1, K_2, K_3, K_4	19	K_{21}	90
K_5, K_6, K_7	20	K_{22}	122
K_8, K_9	21	K_{23}	123
K_{10}	22	K_{24}	124
K_{11}, K_{12}	23	K_{25}	62
K_{13}	31	K_{26}, K_{27}	94
K_{14}	32	K_{28}	96
K_{15}	37	K_{29}	78
K_{16}	47	K_{30}	133
K_{17}	53	K_{31}, K_{32}	135
K_{18}	69	K_{34}, K_{35}	136
K_{19}	71	K_{36}, K_{37}	112
K_{20}	77	K_{38}	113

The cross-references to tables, Rules and appendices are, of course, to those in the Code.

A. Solid rectangular beam

1. Problem

A solid beam, 100 mm x 300 mm deep, of select grade, green blackbutt, fully restrained along the compression flange, is loaded with a 6 kN/m floor live load and a 4 kN/m floor dead load (diagram A). It is supported on 150 mm wide walls having a clear span of 3.5 m. There are three tasks: (a) check the bending strength, (b) check the shear strength and (c) compute the maximum deflection.

Diagram A

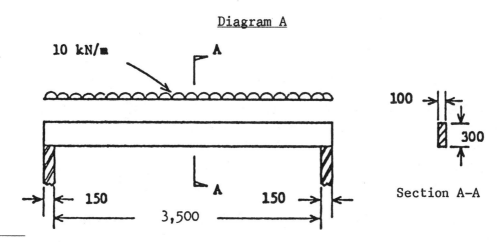

Section A-A

*An officer of CSIRO, Division of Building Research, Melbourne.

2. Solution

Check on bending strength

The stress grade is F22 (table 1.6), $F_b' = 22.0$ MPa (table 2.2.1) and $K_1 = 1.25$ (Rule 1.5.3, table 2.4.1.1). The allowable stress in bending is

$$F_b = F_b' \times K_1 = 22.0 \times 1.25 = 27.5 \text{ MPa}$$

The effective span is $3.5 + 0.15 = 3.65$ m (Rule 3.2.2). The maximum moment is

$$M = WL/8 = \frac{(3.65 \times 10,000) \times 3,650}{8} = 16.6 \times 10^6 \text{ Nmm}$$

The section modulus is

$$Z = BD^2/6 = 100 \times 300^2/6 = 1.5 \times 10^6 \text{ mm}^3$$

Hence, the maximum design working stress is

$$M/Z = \frac{16.6 \times 10^6}{1.5 \times 10^6} = 11.1 \text{ MPa}$$

Check OK since 11.1 < 27.5

Check on shear strength

$F_S' = 1.70$ MPa (table 2.2.1) and $K_1 = 1.25$ (table 2.4.1.1). The allowable shear stress is

$$F_S = F_S' \times K_1 = 1.70 \times 1.25 = 2.12 \text{ MPa}$$

The effective shear span is

$$3.5 - 2 \times 1.5 \times 0.3 = 2.6 \text{ m (Rule 3.2.1)}$$

The maximum shear force is

$$V = (2.6/2) \times (10,000) = 13,000 \text{ N}$$

The maximum design working shear stress is

$$(1.5V)/(BD) = \frac{1.5 \times 13,000 \text{ N}}{100 \times 300} = 0.65 \text{ MPa}$$

Check OK since 0.65 < 2.12

Computation of maximum deflection

$$I = BD^3/12 = 100 \times 300^3/12 = 225 \times 10^6 \text{ mm}^4$$

and $E = 16,000$ MPa (table 2.2.1). For a dead load, $K_2 = 3.0$ (table 2.4.1.2) and $W = 4,000 \times 3.65 = 14,600$ N. Hence, the deflection is

$$\Delta_D = K_2 \times \frac{5}{384} \times \frac{WL^3}{EI} = 3.0 \times \frac{5}{384} \times \frac{14,600 \times 3,650^3}{16,000 \times 225 \times 10^6} = 7.7 \text{ mm}$$

For a live load, $K_2 = 1.0$ and $W = 6,000 \times 3.65 = 21,900$ N. Hence, the deflection is

$$\Delta_L = 7.7 \times \frac{1.0}{3.0} \times \frac{21,900}{14,600} = 3.8 \text{ mm}$$

Total deflection is

$$\Delta = \Delta_D + \Delta_L = 7.7 + 3.8 = 11.5 \text{ mm}$$

B. Glulam beam containing butt joints

1. Problem

A glulam beam of standard grade mountain ash, 50 mm x 240 mm deep in section, is fabricated from 12-20 mm laminations (diagram B). The top eight laminations contain butt joints. The beam spans 5 m with a single lateral restraint at the centre. It is loaded by a central point load of 2 kN dead load and 2 kN floor live load. There are three tasks: (a) check the strength of the continuous laminations, (b) check the fracture strength at the butt joints and (c) specify the minimum spacing of the butt joints.

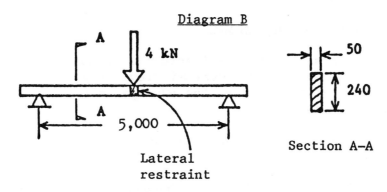

Diagram B

Section A-A

2. Solution

Check on bending strength of continuous laminations

The stress grade is F22 (table 1.6). From Rule 3.2.3, the approximate slenderness coefficient is

$$S_1 = 1.35 \sqrt{\frac{L_{ay} D}{B^2}} \sqrt{1 - (B/D)^2} = 1.35 \sqrt{\frac{2,500 \times 240}{50 \times 50}} \sqrt{1 - (50/240)^2} = 20.7$$

The above estimate is conservative. A more accurate value of S_1 can be obtained from appendix E. Thus, from equation (E3) and table E1,

$$S_1 = \sqrt{\frac{4.8 \times 240 \times 2,500}{50 \times 50 \times 5.5}} = 14.5$$

From table 2.4.8 and Class A straightness, the material coefficient $\rho = 1.03$. Hence, from Rule 3.2.5,

$$K_{12} = \frac{10}{1.03 \times 14.5} = 0.67$$

Also, $K_1 = 1.25$, $K_8 = 1.20$ and $F_b' = 22.0$ MPa. Hence, the allowable working stress in bending is

$$F_b = K_1 \times K_8 \times K_{12} \times F_b' = 1.25 \times 1.16 \times 0.67 \times 22.0 = 22.1 \text{ MPa}$$

The maximum moment is

$$M = \frac{4,000 \times 5,000}{4} = 5.0 \times 10^6 \text{ Nmm}$$

The section modulus is

$$Z = \frac{50 \times 240^2}{6} = 0.48 \times 10^6 \text{ mm}^3$$

Hence, the design working stress is

$$M/Z = \frac{5.0 \times 10}{0.48 \times 10^6} = 10.4 \text{ MPa}$$

Check OK since 10.4 < 22.1

Check on fracture strength of butt joints

The most highly stressed possible fracture location is the lowest butt-jointed lamination at mid-span. As derived previously, the outermost fibre stress at mid-span is 10.4 MPa. Hence, the average tension stress on the critical butt-joint location is

$$f_t = \frac{1.5}{6} \times 10.4 = 2.6 \text{ MPa}$$

The shear force V at this location is 2 kN. Hence, the shear stress across the critical butt joint is

$$f_{sj} = \frac{3}{2} \times \frac{V}{BD} [1 - (\frac{1.5}{6})^2] = \frac{3}{2} \times \frac{2,000}{50 \times 240} [1 - (\frac{1.5}{6})^2] = 0.23 \text{ MPa}$$

Mountain ash is strength group SD3 (table 1.6). Also, F'_{sj} = 2.30 MPA and K_1 = 1.25 (table 2.2.2 and Rule 7.4.2.1(a)(ii)). Hence, the design shear stress is

$$F_{sj} = K_1 \times F'_{sj} = 1.25 \times 2.95 = 2.88 \text{ MPa}$$

The lamination thickness t = 20 mm. Hence, from Rule 7.4.2.1, the check parameter for fracture is

$$\left[\frac{f_t \sqrt{t}}{10 \ F_{sj}}\right] + \left[\frac{f_{sj} \sqrt{t}}{1.7 \ F_{sj}}\right] = \left[\frac{2.6 \sqrt{20}}{10 \times 2.88}\right] + \left[\frac{0.23 \sqrt{20}}{1.7 \times 2.88}\right] = 0.40 + 0.21 = 0.61$$

Check OK since the check parameter < 1.0.

Specification of minimum spacing of butt joints

From Rule 7.4.2.1(c), it can be seen that butt joints within any set of four adjacent laminations may be placed six lamination thicknesses (120 mm) apart.

C. Glulam tie member

1. Problem

A tie is made of four 10 mm thick laminations 100 mm wide, of straight-grained, standard building grade radiata pine (diagram C). The only design

load is a tension axial wind load of 50 kN. The task is to check the tension
strength of the member.

Diagram C

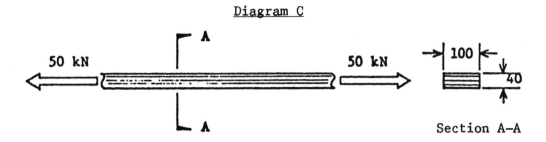

2. Solution

The stress grade is F5 (table 1.6). From Rule 7.3.2.2, it can be seen
that the modification factor for laminating can be taken as either K_8 or K_{20},
whichever is greater. From the appropriate tables, $K_8 = 1.24$, $K_{20} = 1.55$, $K_1 =$
2.0 and $F_t' = 4.3$ MPa. Hence, the allowable working stress in tension is

$$F_t = K_1 \times K_{20} \times F_t' = 2.0 \times 1.55 \times 4.3 = 13.3 \text{ MPa}$$

The applied design working stress in tension is $50,000/(100 \times 40) = 12.5$ MPa.

Check OK since $12.5 < 13.3$

D. Beam-tie

1. Problem

A beam-tie to be used on the north coast of Australia is made of partially
dry, standard engineering grade Douglas fir (diagram D). The size is 40 mm x
250 mm deep and the span is 6 m. It is laterally restrained and loaded at the
third points. The applied load is due to wind only and consists of a lateral
load of 4 kN and an axial tension of 50 kN. The task is to check the strength
of the beam-tie.

Diagram D

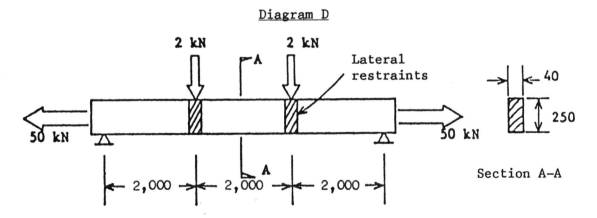

2. Solution

The relevant Rule is Rule 3.5.2. The stress grade is F8. From
Rule 3.2.3, the slenderness coefficient for bending is

$$S_1 = 1.35 \sqrt{\frac{2,000 \times 250}{40 \times 40} \left[1.0 - \left(\frac{40}{250}\right)\right]^2} = 23.6$$

From table 2.4.8 (Class B straightness), the material constant ρ = 0.93. Hence, from Rule 3.2.5, the stability factor is

$$K_{12} = \frac{200}{(0.93 \times 23.6)^2} = 0.41$$

From table 2.4.2, K_4 = 1.10, and from Rule 2.4.3, K_6 = 0.9. Also, F_b' = 8.6 MPa, F_t' = 6.9 MPa and K_1 = 2.0. Hence, the allowable design stress in bending is

$$F_b = K_1 \times K_4 \times K_6 \times K_{12} \times F_b' = 2.0 \times 1.10 \times 0.9 \times 0.41 \times 8.6 = 6.9 \text{ MPa}$$

and the allowable design stress in tension is

$$F_t = K_1 \times K_4 \times K_6 \times F_t' = 2.0 \times 1.10 \times 0.9 \times 6.9 = 13.7 \text{ MPa}$$

Now the design applied stress in tension is

$$f_t = \frac{50,000}{40 \times 250} = 5.0 \text{ MPa}$$

The nominal applied bending moment is

$$M_{nom} = 2,000 \times 2,000 = 4.0 \times 10^6 \text{ Nmm}$$

Also, E = 9,100 and

$$I = \frac{40 \times 250^3}{12} = 52.1 \times 10^6 \text{ mm}^4$$

Deflection due to the nominal bending moment is

$$\Delta_{nom} = \frac{23}{1,296} \frac{WL^3}{EI} = \frac{23}{1,296} \times \frac{4,000 \times 6,000^3}{9,100 \times 52.1 \times 10^6} = 33 \text{ mm}$$

A conservative estimate of the reduction in bending moment due to axial tension force is

$$M_o = T \times \frac{2}{3} \Delta_{nom} = 50,000 \times \frac{2}{3} \times 33 = 1.10 \times 10^6 \text{ Nmm}$$

Hence, the maximum bending moment is

$$M = M_{nom} - M_o = 4.0 \times 10^6 - 1.1 \times 10^6 = 2.9 \times 10^6 \text{ Nmm}$$

The section modulus is

$$Z = \frac{BD^2}{6} = \frac{40 \times 250^2}{6} = 0.416 \times 10^6 \text{ mm}^3$$

Hence, the maximum applied design working stress in bending is

$$f_b = \frac{M}{Z} = \frac{2.9 \times 10^6}{0.416 \times 10^6} = 6.96 \text{ MPa}$$

The applied design tension stress is

$$f_t = \frac{50,000}{40 \times 250} = 5.0 \text{ MPa}$$

The following two checks on strength are specified in Rule 3.5.2:

Check No. 1

$$0.8 \, f_b + f_t = 0.8 \times 6.96 + 5.0 = 10.6 \text{ MPa}$$

Check OK since 10.6 < 13.7.

Check No. 2

$$f_b - f_t = 6.96 - 5.0 = 1.96 \text{ MPa}$$

Check OK since 1.96 < 6.9.

E. Solid column

1. Problem

A flat-ended column of dry, building grade Victorian hardwood is 5 m long and 150 mm x 25 mm in section (diagram E). It has lateral supports every 0.5 m to resist buckling about the minor axis. It has been designed to take a dead load of 10 kN and a roof live load of 3 kN. The task is to check the strength of the column.

Diagram E

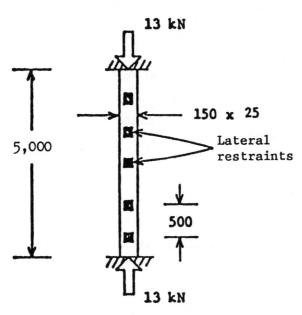

2. Solution

The relevant Rule is Rule 3.3. The stress grade is F14 and the effective length factor $K_{13} = 0.7$. The slenderness coefficient for bending about the major axis is

$$S_2 = \frac{K_{13}L}{D} = \frac{0.7 \times 5,000}{150} = 23$$

The slenderness coefficient for bending about minor axis is

$$S_3 = \frac{L_{ay}}{B} = \frac{500}{25} = 20$$

Since $S_2 > S_3$, the effective slenderness coefficient S of this column is taken to be 23. From table 2.4.8, Class B straightness, the material constant $\rho = 1.09$. Hence, from Rule 3.35, the stability factor is

$$K_{12} = \frac{200}{(1.09 \times 23)^2} = 0.32$$

Furthermore, $F_c' = 10.5$ MPa and $K_1 = 1.35$ (i.e. five-day duration of load, see Rule 1.5.3). Hence, the allowable design compression stress is

$$F_c' = K_1 \times K_{12} \times F_c = 1.35 \times 0.32 \times 10.5 = 4.5 \text{ MPa}$$

The applied design working stress is

$$f_c = \frac{13,000}{150 \times 25} = 3.5 \text{ MPa}$$

Check OK since 3.5 < 4.5

F. Beam-column

1. Problem

A beam-column is made of select engineering grade, dry radiata pine (diagram F). The beam spans 6 m and has lateral restraints at 2 m centres. The section size is 50 mm x 200 mm deep. The maximum axial load is 12 kN, of which 75 per cent is live load, and the maximum bending moment is 0.5×10^6 Nmm, of which 25 per cent is live load. The task is to check the strength of the beam-column.

Diagram F

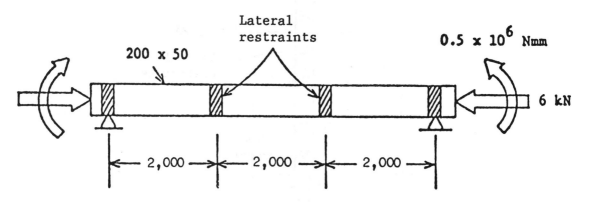

2. Solution

The relevant Rule is Rule 3.5.1 and the stress grade is F11.

Bending parameters

From Rule 3.2.3, the slenderness coefficient is

$$S_1 = 1.35 \sqrt{\frac{2,000 \times 200}{50 \times 50}} \sqrt{1 - \left(\frac{50}{200}\right)^2} = 16.9$$

From table 2.4.8, the material constant $\rho = 1.07$. Hence, from Rule 3.2.4, the stability factor is

$$K_{12} = \frac{10}{1.07 \times 16.9} = 0.55$$

Also, $F_b' = 11.0$ MPa and $K_1 = 1.25$. Hence, the permissible applied design bending stress if no axial load is present is

$$F_b = K_1 \times K_{12} \times F_b' = 1.25 \times 0.55 \times 11.0 = 7.55 \text{ MPa}$$

The section modulus is

$$Z = \frac{BD^2}{6} = \frac{50 \times 200^2}{6} = 0.33 \times 10^6 \text{ mm}^3$$

Hence, the design applied working stress is

$$f_b = \frac{M}{Z} = \frac{0.5 \times 10^6}{0.33 \times 10^6} = 1.5 \text{ MPa}$$

Axial load parameters

$F_c' = 8.3$ MPa and $K_1 = 1.25$. The allowable stress in compression for a stub column is

$$F_c = K_1 \times F_c' = 8.3 \times 1.25 = 10.4 \text{ MPa}$$

The nominal applied axial working stress is

$$f_c = \frac{P}{A} = \frac{6,000}{200 \times 50} = 0.6 \text{ MPa}$$

From Rule 3.3.3, the slenderness coefficient S_2 for buckling about the major axis is $6,000/200 = 30$.

Flom table 2.4.8, the material constant $\rho = 0.97$. Hence, from Rule 3.3.5, the stability factor for buckling about the major axis is

$$K_{12(x)} = \frac{200}{(0.97 \times 30)^2} = 0.236$$

Thus, the allowable stress in compression for buckling about the major axis is

$$F_{cx} = K_1 \times K_{12(x)} \times F_c' = 1.25 \times 0.236 \times 8.3 = 2.44 \text{ MPa}$$

The slenderness coefficient S_3 for buckling about the minor axis is $2,000/50 = 40$. Again, the material constant $\rho = 0.97$. Hence, from Rule 3.35, the stability factor is

$$K_{12(y)} = \frac{200}{(0.97 \times 40)^2} = 0.132$$

Thus, the allowable stress in compression for buckling about the minor axis is

$$F_{cy} = K_1 \times K_{12(y)} \times F_c' = 1.25 \times 0.132 \times 8.3 = 1.37 \text{ MPa}$$

Load interaction effects

For the check parameter in Rule 3.5.1, the following constants apply: $r_b = 0.25$, $r_c = 0.75$ and $K_{14} = 0.5$. Hence, the check parameter is

$$\frac{f_b}{F_b} + \frac{f_c}{F_{cx}} + \frac{f_c}{F_{cy}} + K_{14}\left(\frac{1 + r_c}{1 \times r_b} \times \frac{f_b f_c}{F_b F_{cx}}\right) - \frac{f_c}{F_c}$$

$$= \frac{1.5}{7.55} + \frac{0.6}{2.44} + \frac{0.6}{1.37} + \frac{0.5 \times 1.75 \times 1.5 \times 0.6}{1.25 \times 7.55 \times 2.44} - \frac{0.6}{10.4}$$

$$= 0.20 + 0.25 + 0.44 + 0.03 - 0.06 = 0.86$$

Check OK since check parameter < 1.0.

G. Floor grid system

1. Problem

A floor grid is made up of building grade, green river red gum (diagram G). The five primary beams are 100 mm x 400 mm deep in section and are placed at 1 m centres and span 5 m. The crossing members are 100 mm x 100 mm at 500 mm centres. The effects of dead load are assumed to be negligible. The task is to check that the floor can carry a central point load of 50 kN for a one-day duration.

Diagram G

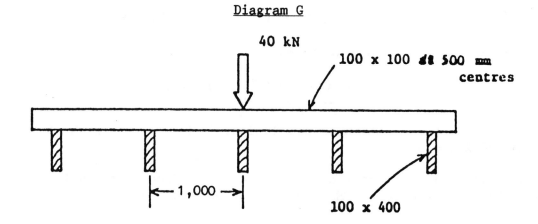

2. Solution

The relevant Rules are Rules 2.4.5.2 and 3.2.7, and the stress grade is F7. The moment of inertia of the primary beams is

$$I_B = \frac{100 \times 400^3}{12} = 532 \times 10^6 \text{ mm}^4$$

and that for the crossing members is

$$I_C = \frac{100 \times 100^3}{12} = 8.34 \times 10^6 \text{ mm}^4$$

Hence, the parameter a in Rule 3.2.7 is

$$\frac{1}{9} \times \frac{532}{8.34} \times \left(\frac{1}{5}\right)^3 = 0.057$$

Hence, the parameter C_4 is

$$\frac{1 + 144 \times 0.057 + 448 \times 0.057 \times 0.057}{5 + 272 \times 0.057 + 448 \times 0.057 \times 0.057} = 0.49$$

Hence, the effective point load is

$$P_{eff} = C_4 P = 0.49 \times 40 = 19.6 \text{ kN}$$

Thus, the maximum moment is

$$M = \frac{19,600 \times 5,000}{4} = 24.5 \times 10^6 \text{ Nmm}$$

The section modulus of the primary members is

$$Z = \frac{BD^2}{6} = \frac{100 \times 400^2}{6} = 2.67 \times 10^6$$

Hence, the design applied bending stress is

$$f_b = \frac{M}{Z} = \frac{24.5 \times 10^6}{2.67 \times 10^6} = 9.2 \text{ MPa}$$

From Rule 2.4.5.2, the grid factor is

$$K_9 = 1.0 + (1.26 - 1.0) \left[1.0 - 2(\tfrac{1}{5})\right] = 1.16$$

Also, the duration factor $K_1 = 1.4$. The allowable design applied bending stress is

$$F_b = K_1 \times K_9 \times F_b' = 1.4 \times 1.16 \times 6.9 = 11.2 \text{ MPa}$$

Check OK since 9.2 < 11.2.

H. Notched beam

1. Problem

A deep laminated beam is fabricated of imported ramin and notched to a depth of 50 mm at a distance 0.5 m from one support (diagram H). The beam is of 100 mm x 500 mm deep sections, spans 8 m and carries a combined distributed dead and live load of 1 kN/m. The task is to check that the fracture strength is satisfactory.

Diagram H

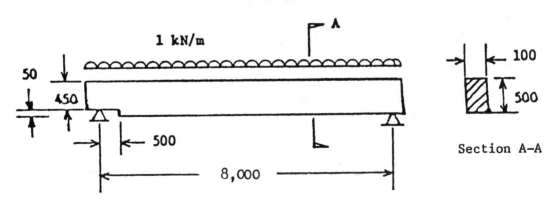

2. Solution

The relevant Rule is Rule 3.2.6 and the strength group is SD5. From table 2.2.2, the basic working stress for shear at the joint details, F_{sj}', is 2.05 MPa. The permissible design working stress in shear at the joints is

$$F_{sj} = K_1 \times F_{sj}' = 1.25 \times 2.05 = 2.56 \text{ MPa}$$

The bending moment at the notch section is

$$M = (1,000 \times 4) \times 500 - (1,000 \times 0.5) \times 250 = 1.88 \times 10^6 \text{ Nmm}$$

The net section modulus is

$$Z_n = \frac{Bd_n^2}{6} = \frac{100 \times 450^2}{6} = 3.37 \times 10^6 \text{ mm}^3$$

The nominal bending stress at the notch root is

$$f_b = \frac{M}{Z_n} = \frac{1.88 \times 10^6}{3.37 \times 10^6} = 0.56 \text{ MPa}$$

The shear force at the notch section is

$$V = 1,000 \times 4 - 1,000 \times 0.5 = 3,500 \text{ N}$$

The nominal shear stress at the notch section is

$$f_s = \frac{3}{2} \times \frac{V}{Bd_2} = \frac{3}{2} \times \frac{3,500}{100 \times 450} = 0.12 \text{ MPa}$$

The notch constant C_3 from table 3.2.6 is $3.0/\sqrt{500} = 0.134$. The check parameter of Rule 3.2.6. is

$$\frac{0.3 f_b + f_s}{C_3 F_{sj}} = \frac{0.3 \times 0.56 + 0.12}{0.134 \times 2.56} = 0.82$$

Check OK since $0.82 < 1.00$.

I. Nailed joint

1. Problem

A tension joint between three pieces of 75 mm x 25 mm dry yellow stringy-bark is fabricated with twelve 3.75 mm diameter nails (diagram I.1). The nails are placed through pre-bored holes to minimize the risk of splitting. The joint is subject to a dead load of 10 kN and a wind load of 10 kN. There are three tasks: (a) specify the required diameter of the pre-bored holes and the minimum nail spacing and end distances, (b) check the strength of the joint and (c) determine the slip of the joint under the action of the dead load.

Diagram I.1

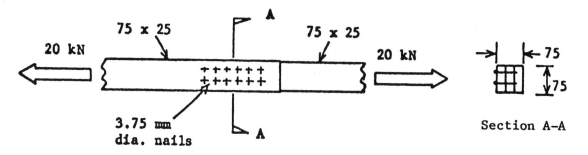

2. Solution

Specification of data

Diameter of pre-bored holes

From Rule 4.2.1.2(j), the required diameter of the pre-bored hole is 0.8 x 3.75 $\simeq$ 3.0 mm.

Minimum spacing and end distances (diagram I.2)

Diagram I.2

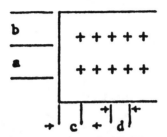

From table 4.2.1.3: a > 11 mm, b > 19 mm, c > 38 mm and d > 38 mm.

Check on strength of joint

The relevant Rule is Rule 4.2. From table 4.1.1, the joint group is J2. From table 4.2.1.1, the basic lateral load per nail, P_B', is 530 N. Also, K_1 = 2.0 and K_{15} = 0.9. From Rule 4.2.1.2(a), the factor for seasoning, K_{seas}, is 1.35. From Rule 4.2.1.2(d), the factor for double shear, K_{ds}, is 2.0. From Rule 4.2.1.2(h)(ii), the factor for inadequate penetration of nails into wood is

$$K_{pen} = \frac{t}{10D_a} = \frac{25}{10 \times 3.75} = 0.68$$

Hence, the allowable design load is

$$P_B = 12 \times K_1 \times K_{15} \times K_{seas} \times K_{ds} \times K_{pen} \times P_B'$$

$$= 12 \times 2.0 \times 0.9 \times 1.35 \times 2.0 \times 0.68 \times 530 = 21,000 \text{ N} = 21 \text{ kN}$$

Check OK since 20 < 21.

Determination of joint slip under dead load

The relevant portion of the Code is appendix H2. The basic lateral load for a nail in green timber is

$$P_B = K_{ds} \times K_{pen} \times P_B' = 2.0 \times 0.68 \times 530 = 720 \text{ N}$$

Also, δ_i = 0, K_{23} = 1.25, K_{24} = 5.0 and P = 10,000/12 = 830 N. Hence, the slip under dead load is

$$\delta = \delta_i + \frac{K_{24}}{9} \times \left(\frac{P}{K_{23} P_B}\right)^2 = 0 + \frac{5}{9} \times \left(\frac{830}{1.25 \times 720}\right)^2 = 0.48 \text{ mm}$$

J. Bolted joint

1. Problem

A joint at the heel of a truss is made with a single M24 (24 mm diameter) bolt (diagram J.1). The timber is green jarrah of the sizes shown. The total dead plus live load, together with the truss support, is shown. There are four tasks: (a) specify the minimum edge distances for a M24 bolt, (b) check the strength of the bolt connection, (c) check the shear capacity of the tie to withstand the effects of the eccentric support, and (d) check the bearing capacity of the tie to withstand the support force.

Diagram J.1

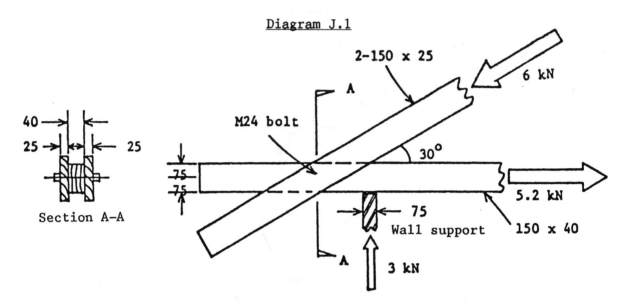

2. Solution

Specification of minimum edge distances (diagram J.2)

The relevant Rule is Rule 4.4.2.6(c).

Diagram J.2

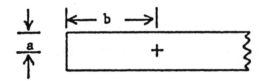

For loading parallel to the grain, a > 50 mm and b > 200 mm for tension member and > 124 mm for compression member. For loading perpendicular to the grain, a > 100 mm and b is not specified. For intermediate values, use interpolation by Hankinson's formula.

Check on strength of the bolt connection

Capacity of bolt to transfer load to compression member

The joint group is J3. From table 4.4.1.1(c), the basic allowable load parallel to the grain, P_B', is 4,790 N and $K_1 = 1.25$. From table 4.4.1.1(a), the bolt capacity is

$$2P_B' \times K_1 = 2 \times 4,790 \times 1.25 = 11,900 \text{ N} = 11.9 \text{ kN}$$

Check OK since 6.0 < 11.9.

Capacity of bolt to transfer load to tension member

It is to be noted that the bolt bears at an angle of 30° to grain. From tables 4.4.1.1(a), 4.4.1.1(c), 4.4.1.2(a) and 4.4.1.2(c), $P_B' = 4,790$ N, $Q_B' = 1,500$ N and $K_1 = 1.25$. The allowable applied design load parallel to the grain is

$$P_B = 2 \times K_1 \times P_B' = 2 \times 1.25 \times 4,790 = 11,900 \text{ N}$$

The allowable applied design load perpendicular to the grain is

$$Q_B = 2 \times K_1 \times Q_B' = 2 \times 1.25 \times 1,500 = 3,750 \text{ kN}$$

From Rule 4.4.1.3, Hankinson's formula for load at 30° to the grain is

$$N_{30} = \frac{11,900 \times 3,750}{11,900 \times \sin^2 30° + 3,750 \times \cos^2 30°} = 7,706 \text{ N}$$

Check OK since 6,000 < 7,706.

Check on shear capacity of tie

The relevant Rule is Rule 4.4.2.7. The shear force is 3 kN and the applied nominal shear stress is

$$f_S = \frac{3}{2} \times \frac{V}{Bd_S} = \frac{3}{2} \times \frac{3,000}{40 \times 75} = 1.5 \text{ MPa}$$

The strength group of green jarrah is S4 and, from table 2.2.2, $F_{sj}' = 1.45$ MPa and $K_1 = 1.25$. Hence, the allowable applied design shear stress is

$$F_{sj} = K_1 \times F_{sj}' = 1.25 \times 1.45 = 1.8 \text{ MPa}$$

Check OK since 1.5 < 1.8.

Check on bearing capacity of tie

The strength group is S4. From tables 2.2.2 and 2.4.4, $F_P' = 3.3$ MPa, $K_1 = 1.25$ and $K_7 = 1.15$. The allowable design bearing stress is

$$F_P = K_1 \times K_7 \times F_P' = 1.25 \times 1.15 \times 3.3 = 4.7 \text{ MPa}$$

The applied design bearing stress is

$$f_P = \frac{3,000}{75 \times 40} = 1.0 \text{ MPa}$$

Check OK since 1.0 < 4.7.

K. Split ring connector joint

1. Problem

Five pairs of 102 split ring connectors are used to form a tension joint between two 250 mm x 50 mm pieces and a 250 mm x 75 mm piece of structural grade No. 1, green karri (diagram K.1). The joint is to be loaded with a live load of 100 kN and a dead load of 150 kN. There are four tasks: (a) check the load capacity of the connectors, (b) check the load capacity of the timber, (c) specify the minimum spacing and end distances of the connectors and (d) determine the joint slip due to the dead load.

<u>Diagram K.1</u>

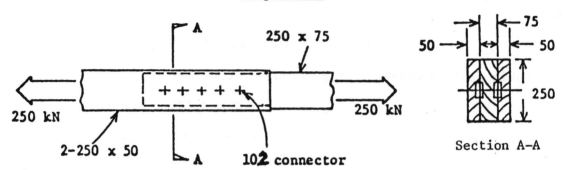

2. Solution

Check on load capacity of connectors

The joint group is J2. From table 4.6.2, the basic allowable load P_B' for a connector is 26.7 kN. Also, K_1 = 1.25 and K_{16} = 0.95. The allowable design load for the joint is

$$W = 10 \times K_1 \times K_{16} \times P_B' = 10 \times 1.25 \times 0.95 \times 26.7 = 317 \text{ kN}$$

The design working load is 250 kN.

Check OK since 250 < 317.

Check on load capacity of timber

The stress grade is F17, F_t' = 14.0 MPa and K_1 = 1.25. The allowable design working stress in tension is

$$F_t = K_1 \times F_t' = 1.25 \times 14.0 = 17.5 \text{ MPa}$$

From table 4.6.4, the net section of the central 250 mm x 75 mm member is

$$A_{net} = (250 \times 75) - (2 \times 1{,}450) = 15{,}800 \text{ mm}^2$$

Hence, the allowable design load is

$$W_{all} = F_t \times A_{net} = 17.5 \times 15{,}800 = 276{,}000 \text{ N} = 276 \text{ kN}$$

Check OK since 250 < 276.

Specification of minimum spacing and end distances (diagram K.2)

The relevant table is table 4.6.4.

Diagram K.2

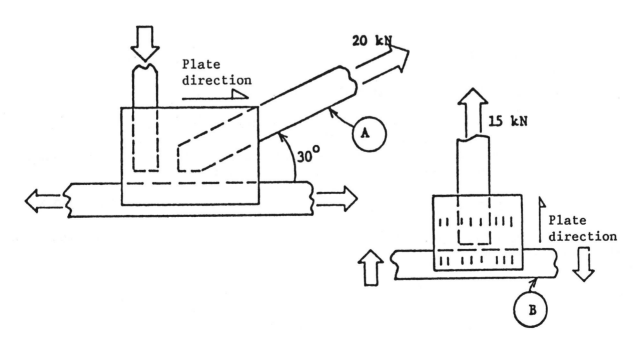

Determination of joint slip due to dead load

The relevant information is in appendix H2: $K_{24} = 4.0$, $K_{23} = 1.0$, $P_B = 26.7$ kN and $n = 5$. Also,

$$P = \frac{250}{10} = 25.0 \text{ kN}$$

Hence,

$$\delta = \frac{1}{2\sqrt{n}} + \frac{K_{24}}{1.2\ K_{23}} \times \frac{P}{P_B} = \frac{1}{2\sqrt{5}} + \frac{4.0 \times 25.0}{1.2 \times 1.0 \times 26.7} = 3.34 \text{ mm}$$

L. Toothed metal plate connector joints

1. Problem

Two joints of dry hoop pine are connected by GN40 toothed metal plates (diagram L). The joint configuration and total dead plus wind loads are as shown. It is to be noted that a nail plate is placed on each side of the joint. Also, two angles are involved: the angle of the load to the grain of the wood and the angle of the plate teeth to the grain of the wood. Further, Rule 4.8.3.6 states that teeth located within 12 mm of the end and 6 mm of the edge of a member are to be considered ineffective. There are three tasks: (a) determine the number of effective teeth that are required for member A, (b) check the strength of the steel plate to hold member A and (c) determine the number of effective teeth that are required for member B.

Diagram L

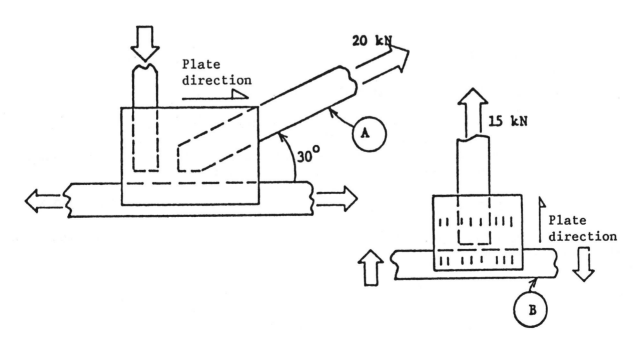

2. Solution

Determination of the number of teeth required for member A

The relevant Rule is Rule 4.8. The joint group is J4. From table 4.8.2 and Rule 4.8.3.4, the basic working load for a tooth at an angle of 30° to the grain is

$$P_B' = \frac{245 \times 180}{245 \times 0.25 + 180 \times 0.75} = 225 \text{ N}$$

Also, $K_1 = 2.0$. From Rule 4.8.3.3, the factor for seasoning, K_{seas}, is 1.25. Hence, the allowable load per tooth is

$$P_B = K_1 \times K_{seas} \times P_B' = 2.0 \times 1.25 \times 225 = 563 \text{ N}$$

Hence, the required number of teeth is 20,000/563 = 36, i.e. 18 teeth on each side.

Check on strength of steel plate to hold member A

From table 4.8.4.7 and Hankinson's formula, the basic allowable load per inch in tension is

$$P_S' = \frac{175 \times 120}{175 \times 0.25 + 120 \times 0.75} = 157 \text{ N}$$

With a factor of 1.25 for wind (see Rule 4.8.3.2), the tension width required is

$$\ell_t = \frac{20,000}{1.25 \times 157} = 102 \text{ mm}$$

that is, 51 mm per plate. Similarly, from table 4.8.4.7, the required shear length is

$$\ell_S = \frac{20,000}{1.25 \times 85} = 188 \text{ mm}$$

that is, 94 mm per plate.

Check OK since required width of 51 mm and overlap of 94 mm is easily obtained.

Determination of the number of teeth required for member B

From table 4.8.2, the basic working load per tooth for a load acting perpendicular to the grain, P_B', is 180 N. $K_1 = 2.0$ and $K_{seas} = 1.25$. From Rule 4.8.3.5, the factor for a load to act perpendicular to the grain, K_{perp}, is 0.8. Hence, the allowable design load per tooth is

$$P_B = K_1 \times K_{seas} \times K_{perp} \times P_B' = 2.0 \times 1.25 \times 0.8 \times 180 = 360 \text{ N}$$

Hence, the required number of teeth is 15,000/360 = 42, that is, 21 teeth on each side of the member.

M. Plywood plate

1. Problem

A seven-ply radiata pine plywood plate, stress grade F8, thickness 17 mm, is to be used in a location where the equilibrium moisture content (emc) is 18 per cent (diagram M). The plate spans 600 mm and carries a dead load of 4,000 Pa. There are three tasks: (a) determine the long-term deflection of the plywood, (b) check the bending strength of the plywood and (c) check the shear strength of the plywood.

Diagram M

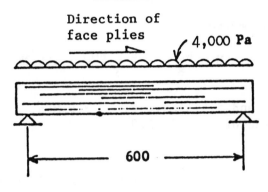

2. Solution

Determination of deflection of plywood

For a strip 1 mm wide, the moment of inertia of plies parallel to the span is

$$I_{par} = \frac{17^3}{12}[1 - (5/7)^3 - (3/7)^3] = 119 \text{ mm}^4$$

$$I_{perp} = \frac{17^3}{12}[(5/7)^3 - (3/7)^3 + (1/7)^3] = 119 \text{ mm}^4$$

From table 5.4.4(a), the effective moment of inertia of the section is

$$I_{eff} = I_{par} + 0.03 \ I_{perp} = 291 + 0.03 \times 119 = 295 \text{ mm}^4$$

From table 5.2, table 5.4.2 and Rule 5.4.2, the elasticity of the plywood, E, taking into consideration the emc, is 9,100 x 0.9 = 8,200 MPa. Also, G = 455 x 0.8 = 364 MPa. From table 2.4.1.2, the creep factor K_2 is 2.3. The total load on a 1 mm wide strip is

$$W = 0.6 \times 0.001 \times 4,000 = 2.4 \text{ N}$$

Hence, the bending deflection under dead load is

$$\Delta_B = K_2 \times \frac{5}{384} \times \frac{WL^3}{EI} = 2.3 \times \frac{5}{384} \times \frac{2.4 \times 600^3}{8,200 \times 295} = 6.5 \text{ mm}$$

The effective area in shear, A_{sh}, is 17 mm². Hence, the shear deflection is

$$\Delta_S = K_2 \times \frac{3}{20} \times \frac{WL}{A_{sh}G} = 2.3 \times \frac{3}{20} \times \frac{2.4 \times 600}{17 \times 364} = 0.1 \text{ mm}$$

The total deflection is

$$\Delta = \Delta_B + \Delta_S = 6.5 + 0.1 = 6.6 \text{ mm}$$

A simple method of computing I_{eff} is given in appendix M. From table M1, $K_{35} = 0.066$. Hence, from equation (M2),

$$I_{eff} = 0.066 \times 17^3 = 325 \text{ mm}^4$$

(There appears to have been an error in tabulating the value of $K_{35} = 0.066$.)

Check on bending strength

The applied bending moment is

$$M = \frac{WL}{8} = \frac{2.4 \times 600}{8} = 180 \text{ Nm}$$

From tables 5.2, 5.4.2 and 5.4.4(a), $F_b' = 8.6$ MPa, $K_{18} = 0.8$ and $K_{19} = 0.85$. The duration of load factor, K_1, is 1.0. Hence, the allowable design bending moment is

$$M_{all} = \frac{K_1 \times K_{18} \times K_{19} \times F_b' \times I_{par}}{y_{max}} = \frac{1.0 \times 0.8 \times 0.85 \times 8.6 \times 291}{0.5 \times 17} = 200 \text{ Nm}$$

Check OK since $180 < 200$.

A simple method of computing M_{all} is to use equation M1 in appendix M:

$$M_{all} = K_1 \times K_{18} \times K_{35} \times F_b \times t_w^2 = 1.0 \times 0.8 \times 0.101 \times 8.6 \times 17^2 = 200 \text{ NM}$$

Check on shear strength

$K_1 = 1.0$, and, from tables 5.2, 5.4.2 and 5.4.4(b), $F_S' = 1.58$ MPa and $K_{18} = 0.8$. Hence, the allowable design working stress in shear is

$$F_S = \frac{3}{8} (K_1 \times K_{18} \times F_S') = \frac{3}{8} \times 1.0 \times 0.8 \times 1.58 = 0.475 \text{ MPa}$$

The design working shear stress is

$$f_S = \frac{3}{2} \times \frac{V}{BD} = \frac{3}{2} \times \frac{1.2}{1.0 \times 17} = 0.106 \text{ MPa}$$

Check OK since $0.106 < 0.475$.

N. Plywood box beam

1. Problem

A box beam is fabricated by gluing 12 mm thick, five-ply, F8 stress grade radiata pine plywood to 150 mm x 50 mm flanges of dry, select grade messmate (diagram N.1). The depth of the beam is 800 mm and the span is 9 m. Both loads and lateral restraints are applied at the third points. The load is 20 kN dead load and 10 kN live load. There are four tasks: (a) determine the maximum deflection of the beam, (b) check the shear connection of the web to the flanges, (c) check the bending strength of the beam and (d) check the shear strength of the beam.

Diagram N.1

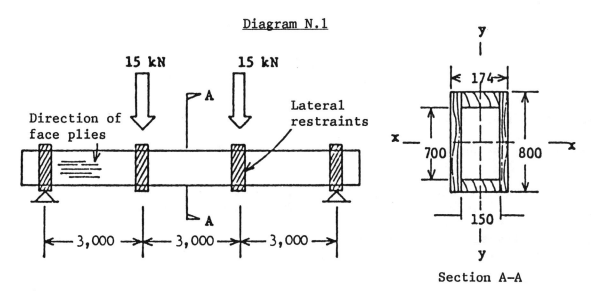

Section A-A

2. Solution

Here, K_1 = 1.25, with K_2 = 2.0 for dead load and K_2 = 1.0 for live load. For dry messmate flanges, and from tables 1.6 and 2.2.1, the stress grade is F27, F'_t = 22.0 MPa, F'_c = 20.5 MPa, E = 18,500 MPa and G = 18,500/15 = 1,230 MPa. For this radiata pine plywood, table 5.2 gives F'_S = 1.58 MPa, E = 9,100 MPa and G = 455 MPa. The box beam may be transformed in terms of equivalent solid messmate as follows (diagram N.2):

The effective thickness of the plywood for computing the moment of inertia is

$$12 \times \frac{2}{3} \times \frac{9,100}{18,500} \cong 4 \text{ mm}$$

The effective thickness of the plywood for computing the torsion modulus is

$$12 \times \frac{455}{1,230} \cong 4.4 \text{ mm}$$

Diagram N.2

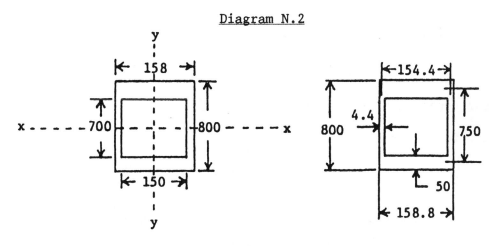

  (a) For moment of inertia   (b) For St. Venant torsion

The transformation to equivalent messmate stringybark cross-sections is as follows:

$$I_x = \frac{1}{12}[158 \times 800^3 - 150 \times 700^3] = 2.44 \times 10^9 \text{ mm}^4$$

$$I_y = \frac{1}{12}[158^3 \times 800 - 150^3 \times 700] = 0.067 \times 10^9 \text{ mm}^4$$

$$J = \frac{2 \times (154.4 \times 750)^2}{(750/4.4) + 154.4} = 0.154 \times 10^9 \text{ mm}^4$$

Determination of deflection of beam

The deflection due to bending caused by dead load is

$$\Delta_{B(D)} = K_2 \times \frac{23}{1,296} \times \frac{WL^3}{EI_x} = 2.0 \times \frac{23}{1,296} \times \frac{20,000 \times 9,000^3}{18,500 \times 2.44 \times 10} = 11.5 \text{ mm}$$

The nominal shear stress due to dead load is

$$\gamma_D = \frac{10,000}{2 \times 700 \times 12} = 0.595 \text{ MPa}$$

The nominal shear strain due to dead load is

$$Y_D = K_2 \times \frac{Y_D}{G} = 2.0 \times \frac{0.595}{455} = 0.0026$$

Hence, the deflection due to shear caused by dead load is

$$\Delta_{S(D)} = \frac{L}{3} \times Y_D = 3,000 \times 0.0026 = 7.8 \text{ mm}$$

Hence, the total deflection under dead load is

$$\Delta_D = \Delta_{B(D)} + \Delta_{S(D)} = 11.5 + 7.8 = 19.3 \text{ mm}$$

For computing the deflection under live load, $K_7 = 1.0$ and $W = 10$ kN. Hence, the deflection under live load is

$$\Delta_L = \frac{1.0}{2.0} \times \frac{10}{20} \times \Delta_D = 4.60 \text{ mm}$$

Hence, the total maximum deflection is

$$\Delta = \Delta_D + \Delta_L = 19.3 + 4.8 = 24.1 \text{ mm}$$

Check on shear connection of web to flanges

The shear force per millimetre of flange is

$$v = \frac{V}{d} = \frac{15,000}{700} = 21 \text{ N/mm}$$

The total plywood contact area per millimetre run of flange is

$$A_{con} = 50 \times 2 = 100 \text{ mm}^2$$

Hence, the design rolling shear stress is

$$f_{rs} = \frac{v}{A_{con}} = \frac{21}{100} = 0.21 \text{ MPa}$$

From table 5.4.4(b), the permissible working stress in rolling shear is

$$F_{rs} = 0.19 \times K_1 \times F_S' = 0.19 \times 1.25 \times 1.58 = 0.38 \text{ MPa}$$

Check OK since 0.21 < 0.38.

Check on bending strength of beam

From equation (E4) and table E1 in appendix E, the Euler buckling load capacity of the beam is

$$M_E = \frac{C_5}{L_{ay}} \times \left(\frac{EI_y \, GJ}{1 - I_y/I_x} \right)^{1/2}$$

$$= \frac{3.1}{3,000} \times \left(\frac{18,500 \times 0.067 \times 10^9 \times 1,230 \times 0.154 \times 10^9}{1 - (0.067/2.44)} \right)^{1/2}$$

$$= 0.506 \times 10^9 \text{ Nmm}$$

Hence, from equation (E1) in appendix E, the slenderness coefficient is

$$S_1 = \left(\frac{1.1 \times EI_x}{M_E y_{max}} \right)^{1/2}$$

$$= \left(\frac{1.1 \times 18,500 \times 2.44 \times 10^9}{0.506 \times 10^9 \times 400} \right)^{1/2} = 15.6$$

From table 2.4.8, the material constant ρ for the messmate (Class A straightness) is 1.10. From Rule 3.2.5, the stability factor is

$$K_{12} = \frac{10}{1.10 \times 15.6} = 0.58$$

Also, $K_1 = 1.25$ and $K_{11} = 0.85$. The allowable stress is lowest in the compression flange. Hence, the allowable nominal stress due to bending is

$$F_b = K_1 \times K_{11} \times K_{12} \times F_c' = 1.25 \times 0.85 \times 0.57 \times 20.5 = 12.6 \text{ MPa}$$

The maximum applied design bending moment is

$$M = 15,000 \times 3,000 = 45.0 \times 10^6 \text{ Nmm}$$

The maximum applied working stress in bending is

$$f_b = \frac{(M)(y_{max})}{I_{max}} = \frac{45.0 \times 10^6 \times 400}{2.62 \times 10^9} = 6.9 \text{ MPa}$$

Check OK since 7.5 < 12.6.

Check on shear strength of beam

From tables 5.2 and 5.4.4(a), the allowable basic stress in shear, F_S', is 1.58 MPa. From equation (L2) and table L1 in appendix L, the slenderness coefficient of the web in shear is

$$S = 0.8 \ K_{30} \ x \ \frac{a}{t_w} = 0.8 \ x \ 0.38 \ x \ \frac{700}{12} = 17.7$$

The factor 0.8 allows for edge fixing of sheet. The panel is

$$b_{ch} = 1.65 \ x \ 700 = 1,160 \ mm$$

Since 1,160 < 3,000, the modified formula for slenderness coefficient (L3) is not applicable. From table 2.4.8, the material constant for the F8 plywood is 0.92. Hence, from Rule 2.4.8, the stability factor for the web is

$$K_{12} = \frac{10}{0.92 \ x \ 17.7} = 0.615$$

Also, $K_1 = 1.25$ and $F_S' = 1.58$ MPa. Hence, the allowable design shear stress is

$$F_S = K_1 \ x \ K_{12} \ x \ F_S' = 1.25 \ x \ 0.615 \ x \ 1.58 = 1.21 \ MPa$$

The applied design shear stress in plywood webs is

$$f_S = \frac{V}{2t_w d} = \frac{15,000}{2 \ x \ 12 \ x \ 700} = 0.89 \ MPa$$

Check OK since 0.89 < 1.21.

O. Spaced column

1. Problem

The two main shafts of a spaced column are two 150 mm x 25 mm dry alpine ash of building grade (diagram O). These shafts are separated by 50 mm thick packing pieces nailed to the shafts at 700 mm centres. Each packing piece is nailed by six 3.75 mm diameter nails to each shaft. The total column is 3.1 m long and has flat-ended support conditions. The applied axial load is a 2 kN live load and a 3 kN dead load. There are three tasks: (a) check the strength of the spaced column, (b) check the nail strength of the connection between the main shaft and the packing pieces and (c) use the formulae in appendix H to obtain an accurate estimate of the slenderness coefficient S_4 for composite buckling.

Diagram 0

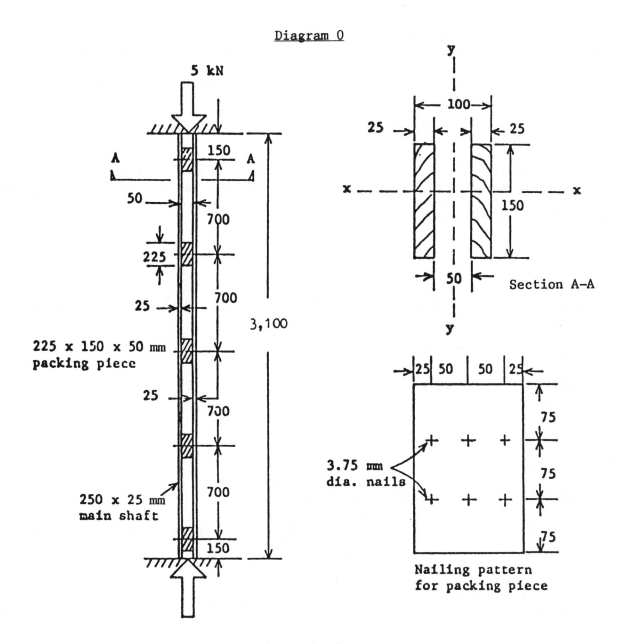

Section A-A

Nailing pattern
for packing piece

3.75 mm
dia. nails

2. Solution

Check on strength of spaced column

For buckling about the y-y axis,

$$I_{net} = \frac{1}{12} \times 150 \times (100^3 - 50^3) = 11.0 \times 10^6 \; mm^4$$

$$A_{net} = 2 \times 150 \times 25 = 7,500 \; mm^2$$

$$K_{13} = 0.7 \; (flat\text{-}ended \; column)$$

$$K_{21} = 3.1 \; (table \; 8.3.4.3)$$

Hence, from Rule 8.3.4.2, the slenderness coefficient is

$$S_4 = \frac{K_{13}K_{21}}{3.5\sqrt{I/A}} = \frac{0.7 \times 3.1 \times 3,100}{3.5\sqrt{11.0 \times 10^6/7,500}} = 50$$

(From Rule 3.3.4, the maximum permissible value of the slenderness coefficient is 50.) The slenderness coefficient of the main shaft between the spacer blocks is 700/50 = 14, so the local buckling of the main shaft does not govern the design. For buckling about the x-x axis, the slenderness coefficient is

$$S_1 = \frac{K_{13}L}{B} = \frac{0.7 \times 3,100}{150} = 14.5$$

Hence, the minimum effective slenderness coefficient for the spaced column is 50. From table 1.6, the stress grade of dry alpine ash is F17. Hence, from table 2.4.8, for Class A straightness, the material coefficient is $\rho = 0.99$ and, from Rule 3.3.5, the stability factor is

$$K_{12} = \frac{200}{(0.99 \times 50)^2} = 0.0815$$

Furthermore, $F_c' = 13.0$ MPa and $K_1 = 1.25$. Hence, the allowable design working stress in compression is

$$F_c = K_1 \times K_{12} \times F_c' \times 0.0815 \times 13.0 = 1.32 \text{ MPa}$$

The applied design working stress in compression is

$$f_c = \frac{5,000}{2 \times 150 \times 25} = 0.67 \text{ MPa}$$

Check OK since 0.67 < 1.32.

Check on nail connection of packing pieces

From Rules 8.3.2 and 8.3.3.6, the design shear force in the spaced column is

$$Q = 0.003 \frac{Lp}{D} = \frac{0.003 \times 3,100 \times 5,000}{100} = 465 \text{ N}$$

and the corresponding shear force that then occurs between a packing piece and the main shaft is

$$V = \frac{QL_S}{2t} = \frac{460 \times 700}{2 \times 75} = 2,170 \text{ N}$$

Hence, the applied design load per nail is

$$P_{nail} = \frac{2,170}{6} = 362 \text{ N}$$

Alpine ash is joint group J3, $P_B' = 450$ N, $K_1 = 1.25$, $K_{15} = 0.94$ and the factor for seasoning, K_{seas}, is 1. Hence, the allowable design load per nail is

$$P_B' = K_1 \times K_{15} \times K_{seas} \times P_B' = 1.25 \times 0.94 \times 1.35 \times 450 = 714 \text{ N}$$

Check OK since 360 < 714.

Use of appendix H to obtain improved estimate of slenderness coefficient S_4

The relevant portion of the Code is appendix H2. Since $K_{23} = 1.25$, $K_{24} = 4$, $P = 360$ and $P_B = 450$, the slip modulus is

$$k = \frac{9 \times (K_{23}P_b)^2}{K_{24}P} = \frac{9 \times (1.25 \times 450)^2}{4 \times 360} = 1,960 \text{ N/mm}$$

Also,

$$\Sigma I_o = 2 \times \frac{150 \times 25^3}{12} = 0.39 \times 10^6 \text{ mm}^4$$

And, from the earlier check on the strength of the spaced column, $I_{net} = 11.0 \times 10^6 \text{ mm}^4$. Hence, the parameter Σ is

$$\frac{\Sigma I_i}{I_{net}} = \frac{0.39}{11.0} = 0.0354$$

With $L_c = 662$, $L_S = 700$ and $L = 3,100$, the parameter μ is

$$\mu = \frac{\pi^2}{12\varepsilon} \times (L/L)^2 \times \frac{L_c}{L_s} = \frac{\pi^2}{12 \times 0.0354} \times (662/3,100)^2 \times \frac{662}{700} = 1.00$$

Given $A_m = 3,750 \text{ mm}^2$ (figure 8.3.1), $s_n = 3,100/(6 \times 5) = 103$, $E = 14,000 \text{ MPa}$ and $K_{22} = 1.0$, the parameter ν is

$$\frac{\pi^2 EA_m s_n K_{22}}{kL^2} = \frac{\pi^2 \times 14,000 \times 3,750 \times 103 \times 1.0}{1,960 \times 3,100 \times 3,100} = 2.86$$

Hence, from equation (H1),

$$K_{21} = \left[\frac{1 + \mu + \nu}{1 + \varepsilon(\mu + \nu)}\right]^{1/2} = \left[\frac{1 + 1.00 + 2.86}{1 + 0.0354(1.00 + 2.86)}\right]^{1/2} = 2.07$$

Hence, from Rule 8.3.4.2, the slenderness coefficient is

$$S_4 = \frac{0.7 \times 2.07 \times 3,100}{\sqrt{3.5 \times 11.0 \times 10^6/7,500}} = 33$$

The slenderness coefficient S_4 obtained by this more reliable computation is 33 as compared with the value of 50 obtained through the use of the approximate value of $K_{21} = 3.1$ from table 8.3.4.3.

P. Test loads

1. Problem

A new type of roof structure, designed to carry a live load of 50 kN and a dead load of 100 kN, is to be fabricated of dry timber. Although an exact structural analysis is too complex to be undertaken, it is clear that the compression members will be the critical members. Because of the use of careful fabrication techniques, the coefficient of variation of these types of structures is conservatively estimated to be 15 per cent. There are two tasks:

(a) In prototype tests on two structures, it was found that it took about 2 hr to apply the test load and the loads at failure were 450 kN and 500 kN. On the basis of these test results, determine if the structure can carry the specified design load of 150 kN;

(b) Determine what would have been the required magnitude of the proof test load if it had been decided to accept structures on the basis of proof tests instead of prototype tests.

2. Solution

Determination of strength based on prototype test results

The relevant Rule is Rule 9.5.4. Also, $K_1 = 1.25$, $K_{26} = 1.1$, $K_{27} = 0.93$ and $K_{28} = 1.6$. Hence, the minimum strength necessary in the prototype test is

$$\frac{2.2 \, K_{26} K_{27} K_{28} {\scriptstyle \Sigma} P}{K_1} = \frac{2.2 \times 1.1 \times 0.93 \times 1.6 \times 150}{1.25} = 430 \text{ kN}$$

Check OK since 450 > 430.

Determination of proof load

From Rule 9.4.1, the necessary proof load is

$$\frac{2.1 \times K_{26} K_{27}}{K_1} (P_D + 1.4 P_L) = \frac{2.1 \times 1.1 \times 0.93}{1.25} (100 + 1.4 \times 50) = 293 \text{ kN}$$

A much finer design can be obtained on the basis of proof testing. This is because proof loads need load factors to account for the variability of loads only; in prototype testing, the load factors are also required to account for the variability of the structure.

VI. WIND RESISTANCE OF TIMBER BUILDINGS

Greg F. Reardon*

Introduction

The design of buildings to resist wind forces is usually less precise than the design for gravity loads. Some of the reasons for this are that although the basic wind design data may reflect the true wind regime of an area, the engineer has to base the design on the presence or absence of other buildings in the vicinity, and he or she is required to make assumptions about the likely state of the building when the gust wind hits.

Design wind velocities are derived from anemometer records accumulated over a period of time. The anemometers are located at airports and possibly at two or three other locations in a large city. Thus there is a high probability that the maximum wind gusts from many storms are not recorded. How- ever, if the anemometer records are for a considerable time span, their accuracy is improved.

The presence or absence of other buildings and topographic features affect the wind environment around a building. For multi-storey buildings this effect can readily be measured using wind tunnel models. For low-rise buildings such as small factories or houses where one standard design may be used for the construction of many buildings in different locations, the site conditions may vary significantly from those assumed by the engineer. Moreover, the engineer's design assumption of internal pressures within a low-rise building can be grossly exceeded if a door is left open or a window broken.

Despite these potential hazards, engineered low-rise buildings have performed well during extreme cyclones [1], but generally domestic buildings do not have a history of resisting wind forces very well. Although most domestic buildings have timber structural members, this poor performance does not necessarily reflect a lack of knowledge of timber engineering. Rather, it point to a lack of engineering input into domestic construction. This situation is changing, however, as more information becomes available on engineered domestic construction [2], [3], [4], [5].

The average annual payout by private insurance companies in Australia for storm and tempest damage is approximately $A 10 million, most of it paid on domestic buildings. The author's investigations of wind damage usually revealed a lack of appreciation of joint details needed to withstand wind forces.

A. Wind action on buildings

Wind velocities

The basic design wind velocity in Australia varies from 37 to 50 m/sec in non-cyclone areas, depending upon location, and is 55 m/sec for cyclone-prone

---

*Technical Director, James Cook University Cyclone Testing Station, Townsville, Queensland, Australia.

areas. These speeds are based on a statistical analysis of the gust wind data collected from anemometer records and represent the gust wind speeds likely to occur on average once in a 50-year period. The basic design velocities for a 25-year period would be less and for a 100-year period, greater.

Eaton [6] lists suggested once-in-50-year design gust velocities for various countries that experience cyclones, based on data collected by the Meteorological Office of the United Kingdom. This information is reproduced in table 10.

Table 10. Once-in-50-years design gust speeds for
some countries that experience hurricanes
(Metres per second)

Country or area	Gust speed
North Indian Ocean	
India	34-61
Sri Lanka	36
South Indian Ocean	
Mauritius	68
Mozambique	31-38
Réunion	57
Rodriguez	90
Western North Pacific	
Hong Kong	71
Japan	27-68
Macau	56
Malaysia	25-35
Philippines	20-69
Republic of Korea	30-55
Taiwan Province	79
Southwest Pacific	
New Caledonia	35-54
Pacific (East) Islands	27-52
Samoa	39
South Atlantic	
Antigua	53
Barbados	53
Bermuda	60
Grenada	45
Jamaica	53
Martinique	44
Mexico	27-60
Panama	26
Puerto Rico	49
St. Barthelemy	53
Trinidad and Tobago	42
Venezuela	29-42

Source: K. J. Eaton, "Buildings and tropical windstorms", Overseas Building Note No. 188, Building Research Establishment, United Kingdom, 1981.

It should be noted that the basic wind velocities discussed so far represent the peak gusts likely to occur on average once in 50 years (50-year-return period). It can be shown mathematically that there is a 63 per cent chance that a peak gust velocity or one even larger will occur during a given 50-year period.

The wind velocity that impacts a building is affected by the degree of shielding offered by surrounding objects. Figure 42A illustrates a building in an exposed terrain where there are few objects to protect the building. By contrast, the similar building in figure 42B is well protected by the other houses and trees surrounding it. Other buildings of similar size in effect slow down the wind to approximately two thirds of the value for exposed terrain.

Figure 42. Exposed terrain and sheltered terrain

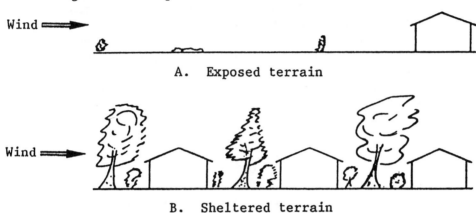

A. Exposed terrain

B. Sheltered terrain

2. External pressures

When the wind approaching from square on hits a building it causes pressure to act in the windward wall and suction (pressure reduction) to act on the other walls and on the roof (for relatively low roof pitches). Figure 43 illustrates this action.

Figure 43. Pressures acting on the external surfaces of a house

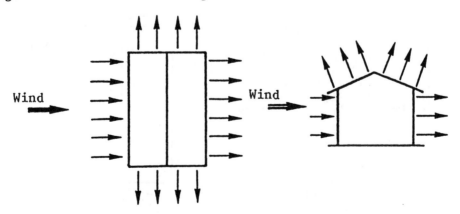

If the wind approaches the building from an oblique angle, the pressure distribution on the front wall is more complex as it is greater towards the edge nearest the wind but may even become a suction at the other edge of the wall.

The pressures caused by wind on a building are easily calculated from the formula

$$p = 0.5 \, \rho V^2 \qquad (1)$$

where ρ is the density of air and V is the velocity of the wind striking the building. The value of ρ varies with both temperature and atmospheric pressure. A value of 1.2 kg/m^3 is used in the Australian Wind Loading Code [7]. This represents an ambient temperature of about 21° C at standard atmospheric pressure (1,013 mbar). Eaton [6] argues that a value of 1.122 kg/m^3 representing 25° C and 960 mbar, may be more realistic when designing for cyclone conditions, to compensate for the higher ambient temperature in tropical areas and the reduced pressure associated with a cyclone. This suggestion would result in a 7.5 per cent reduction in forces.

The forces caused by wind on a surface are not uniform, even when the wind acts square on to the surface. On the windward wall, they tend to be greatest near the centroid of the area and not as great near the edges. This phenomenon is logical because the air at the edges is free to spill around them and therefore is less restricted than the air hitting the centroid. On leeward surfaces the suction increases near the edges. For design purposes, however, it is more convenient to assume that the pressure acting on a surface is uniform. It is normally expressed in the form of a non-dimensional coefficient based on the following equation:

$$C_p(t) = \frac{p(t) - p_0}{0.5 \, \rho \bar{u}^2} \qquad (2)$$

where p_0 is a static (ambient atmospheric) reference pressure and $\bar{u}$ is a mean velocity measured at a convenient reference height. For low-rise buildings, it is usually taken as the height of the eaves. As indicated, $p(t)$, the pressure at a point on the surface, and $C_p(t)$, the pressure coefficient, are both time-dependent. Most design codes, however, adopt a quasi-static approach and use mean pressure coefficient acting on surfaces. Figure 44 shows mean pressure coefficients for a house, obtained from wind tunnel tests [8], with the wind acting square on and at 45°.

Figure 44. Mean external pressure coefficients for wind
acting at 0° and at 45°

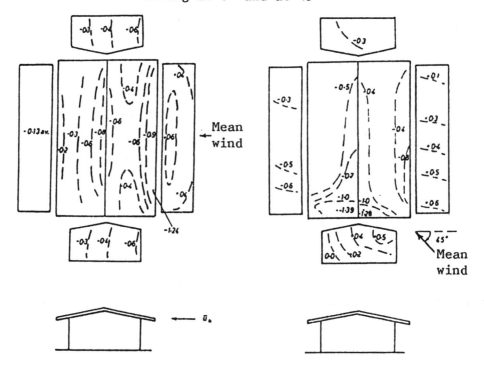

3. Internal pressures

Not only does the wind affect the external surfaces of a building, it can cause severe pressures within a building. Figure 45 illustrates this effect for openings on either the windward or the leeward wall.

Figure 45. Internal pressures due to openings on
the windward and leeward walls

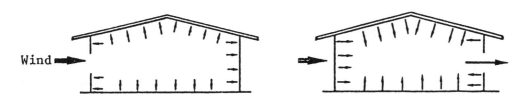

The magnitude of the internal pressure depends upon the ratio of areas of windward and leeward opening. Holmes [9] showed that the mean internal pressure coefficient can be predicted reasonably accurately from the following equation:

$$\bar{C}_{p_i} = \frac{\bar{C}_{p_W}}{1 + (A_L/A_W)^2} + \frac{\bar{C}_{p_L}}{1 + (A_W/A_L)^2} \tag{3}$$

where $\bar{C}_{p_W}$ and $\bar{C}_{p_L}$ are the mean pressure coefficients at the windward and leeward openings, respectively, and A_W and A_L are the areas of the windward and leeward openings.

Holmes also showed from wind tunnel tests that the internal pressure is generated for openings of 5 per cent or more of the total surface area.

B. Design forces

1. Design parameters

In this chapter, design calculations are based on a working stress approach rather than a limit state concept.

As with most engineering designs, the criteria for strength and for serviceability (stiffness) should both be satisfied. The design forces for strength may be different from those for serviceability.

To calculate design forces, a set of design parameters must be established. These parameters include basic design wind velocity, height above ground, degree of exposure, external pressure coefficients, internal pressure coefficients and local pressure factors.

Basic design wind velocities are available from wind loading codes. If such information is not available, the values listed in table 10 may help the designer. In the cyclone-prone areas of Australia, the basic wind velocity is increased by 15 per cent because it was found that the risk of building failure is greater than in the areas not prone to cyclones.

When designing timber buildings for strength, it is usual to use the basic wind velocity related to a 50-year-return period. However, when designing for serviceability, it is more rational to use a 25-year-return period. This concept accepts possible cracking of rigid lining materials by the 50 year design wind, but considers such minor failure to be acceptable because of overall saving in the cost of construction.

Wind speeds increase with height above ground. For a timber-framed building one or two storeys high, a height of 6 m above the ground would be a suitable datum for the wind.

As illustrated in figure 42, the terrain surrounding the building to be designed has a significant effect on the wind that eventually hits the building. For a given initial wind gust, the speed of the wind hitting the house in figure 42B would be approximately two thirds the speed of that hitting the house in 42A.

External pressure coefficients C_{p_e} vary, depending upon wind direction, as shown in figure 44. For design purposes, one coefficient per surface is usually used, but if the surface is large, a number of coefficients may be used. Also, at edges where suction forces can be quite high, an increased pressure coefficient is often used. One way of expressing this increase is as a local pressure factor, which is a multiplier applied to the average pressure coefficient used for areas of high suction.

The internal pressure coefficient C_{p_i} is uniform throughout the building and acts on both ceilings and walls. The magnitude of the internal pressure coefficient depends on the ratio of permeability of the windward wall to permeability of the other walls. The decision that rests with the engineer when calculating design forces is what permeability ratio to design for. If it is anticipated that a window will be broken during a storm, the maximum value of the internal pressure coefficient should be used.

2. Calculation of pressures

The following is an example using values taken from the Australian Loading Code [7].

A timber-framed house is to be designed for a sheltered terrain in the defined cyclone-prone area. To calculate the pressures exerted by the wind on the house, the following values are assumed:

Basic design wind velocity	55 m/s
Cyclonic multiplier	1.15
Terrain category factor (for 6 m height above ground)	0.66
External pressure coefficients*	
Windward wall	+0.8
Side walls	-0.6
Leeward wall	-0.5
Roof	-0.9

---

*Negative pressure coefficients indicate suction acting on the surface.

Internal pressure coefficient   +0.8

Local pressure factor
   Edges of roof and walls   1.5
   Corners of roof   2.0

The following may then be calculated:

Design wind velocity for sheltered terrain = 55 x 1.15 x 0.66 = 42 m/s

Free stream dynamic pressure $(0.5 \rho v^2)$ = 0.5 x 1.2 x 42^2 = 1,058 N/m² = 1.06 kPa

Pressure on windward wall = 0.8 x 1.06 = +0.85 kPa

Pressure on side walls = −0.6 x 1.06 = −0.64 kPa

Pressure on leeward wall = 0.5 x 1.06 = −0.53 kPa

Pressure on roof = −0.9 x 1.06 = −0.95 kPa

Internal pressures = +0.8 x 1.06 = +0.85 kPa

These calculated pressures acting on the various surfaces will be used in the design examples given in sections C and D.

C. Resistance against uplift

1. Timber framing

The timber-framed structure of a house normally has to resist gravity loads. However, if the wind uplift pressure is greater than the gravity loads, the net effect is an uplift force on the building. It is usually assumed that the live load will not be acting when the wind blows.

Timber is a very suitable material for short-duration loading such as wind loading or earthquake loading. The basic working stresses may be increased by 75 per cent for loads of duration of 5 sec or less [10]. Therefore timber members that are designed for strength and stiffness criteria under gravity loading are often suitable for wind loading. Timber structures that consist of a number of members joined to form the structure are more susceptible to damage from uplift loading. In such cases, members acting as ties for gravity loads become struts for uplift. That is, they become columns and need lateral support to prevent them from buckling. A typical example of this action is the bottom chord of a roof truss. Unless lateral support is available from a ceiling membrane, special provision would have to be made to prevent buckling.

The usual weakness against uplift forces in light framed timber construction is the joints. Quite often they are only nominal, enough to keep the timber members in place under gravity loading. An example of this is the joint between stud and plate in domestic construction. This joint is made either by skew nailing from the stud to the plate or by nailing through the plate into the end grain of the studs. In either case the joint is not adequate to transfer the full uplift load into the studs. Therefore, either a suitable jointing medium between stud and plate is needed or another member that can be easily jointed must be introduced to carry the tensile forces generated by the wind uplift. Both of these methods are used extensively in Australia.

2. Design example

A timber-framed house is to be constructed in sheltered terrain in a cyclone-prone area, using unseasoned hardwood of stress grade F11 and joint group J3. It is assumed that factory-fabricated roof trusses are used and that they have been correctly designed. It is also assumed that all timber sizes for wall framing and floor structure have been correctly specified. The exercise is to design the joints for the house, given the following information (dimensions in mm):

Length	14,000
Width	7,000
Wall height	2,400
Eaves	600
Truss spacing	900
Roof batten spacing	900
Roof pitch	10°
Roofing	Corrugated iron
External wall cladding	Brick veneer
Internal wall cladding	Plasterboard

The design pressures calculated in section B.2 will be used in this example. It is assumed that the internal pressure can act on the under-side of the roof sheeting.

(a) Joint between roof batten and roof truss:

Uplift pressure on surface of roofing	= 0.95 kPa
Internal pressure on under-side of roofing	= 0.85 kPa
Hence, total uplift pressure on roofing	= 1.8 kPa
Weight of roofing [11]	= 0.05 kPa
Weight of battens	= 0.05 kPa
Hence, total uplift pressure	= 1.7 kPa
Force on fastener	= 1.7 x 0.9 x 0.9 = 1.4 kN

Since their allowable withdrawal load is 1.7 kN [12], use power-driven 75 x 4.88 mm screws for batten/rafter joints (figure 46).

Figure 46. Batten/rafter joint

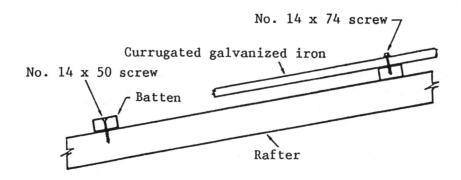

(b) Hold down of roof truss:

Total uplift pressure on roof truss = 1.8 kPa
Estimated weight of truss, battens,
  roofing and ceiling   = 0.37 kPa
Area supported by each truss   = (7 + 2 x 0.6) x 0.9 = 7.4 m^2
Hence, uplift force at support   = 0.5 x 7.4 x 1.43 = 5.3 kN
Allowable stress in M10 bolt in
  tension, through overbatten
  and top plate   = 8.4 kN
Check bearing area beneath bolt
Basic allowable bracing stress for
  S4 timber   = 3.3 MPa [10]
Modification for wind loading,
  partial seasoning   = 3.3 x 1.75 x 1.10 = 6.4 MPa
Washer area required   = 830 mm

Therefore, use 38 mm diameter washer. Figure 47 shows detail.

Figure 47. Roof truss hold down

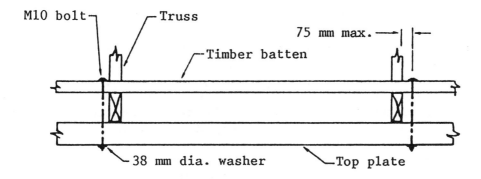

(c) Joint of top plate to studs:

Uplift force from truss   = 5.3 kN
Since calculations show that only
  70 per cent of the uplift force
  will be transferred to any
  individual stud (studs at 450 mm
  spacing), uplift on stud   = 3.7 kN

Since the allowable lift on one TECO Trip-L-Grip is 2 kN [13], use two Trip-L-Grips per stud/top plate connection, as shown in figure 48. The remaining hold-down details can be calculated in a similar manner.

Figure 48. Stud/top plate connection

Use a Trip-L-Grip on opposite corners of each stud

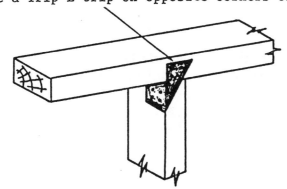

As a point of interest, consider the truss hold-down detail once again. A detail sometimes suggested consists of a steel angle bolted through one leg to the top plate and bolted through the other to the truss. It is not a very good detail, as the bolt to the truss is bearing almost perpendicular to the grain of the timber and thus has a low design load. In fact, calculations using Hankinson's formula [10, Rule 4.41.3] show that even an M16 bolt is not adequate to safely resist the 5.3 kN uplift force.

3. Cyclic loading

The wind gusts associated with thunderstorm and gale activity include only a few gusts of high wind speed, and the total storm is usually over within a relatively short period. With tropical cyclones, the period of gust activity extends for about three hours, depending upon the size and forward speed of the cyclone. During that time, buildings are subjected to thousands of gusts of varying intensity, causing fatigue loading conditions. Timber is not adversely affected by cyclic fatigue loading, but some types of joint and some claddings are. The joints that can be affected are those that incorporate light-gauge metal, such as the framing anchors illustrated in figure 47. Leicester [14] reports a loss of about 30 per cent of initial holding power after 10,000 cycles of load.

Metal roof cladding is also susceptible to fatigue by the amount of cyclic loading occurring during a cyclone. Walker [1] described extensive loss of light-gauge roof sheeting in Darwin during cyclone Tracy. Subsequent research by Morgan and Beck [15] and Beck and Morgan [16] led to the recommendations [17] now used extensively in the testing of roof and wall cladding for cyclone areas in Australia. In summary, the tests require a section of roof sheeting to be loaded without failure to 10,200 cycles in the following manner:

8,000 cycles	0 - 0.625 x Design pressure - 0
2,000 cycles	0 - 0.75 x Design pressure - 0
200 cycles	0 - Design pressure - 0
One application	k x Design pressure

where the value of k is dependent upon the number of replications tested:

No. of replications	K
1	2
2	1.8
5	1.6

Similar recommendations apply to structures or structural elements that may lose strength from cyclic loading, although only one tenth of the number of cycles are necessary, allowing for damping to occur.

D. Resistance against racking forces

1. Racking forces

The action of wind pressure on the windward wall of a building and suction on the leeward wall combine to try to rack the building out of square (figure 49).

Figure 49. Racking action of wind

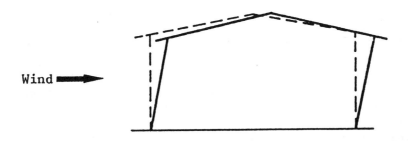

Wind ➡

Using a simplified engineering analysis, half the pressure acting on the windward and leeward walls is transferred directly to the ground while the other half is transferred to the top of the walls. This force at the top of the walls is the racking force.

Using the examples of sections B.2 and C.2 and assuming that the wind is approaching normal to the long wall, the total racking force can be calculated as follows:

Pressure on windward wall   = 0.85 kPa
Area of windward wall   = 14 x 2.4 = 33.6 m^2
Pressure on leeward wall   = -0.53 kPa
Racking force   = 0.5 x 33.6 x (0.85 + 0.53) = 23.2 kN

The racking force must be resisted by bracing walls located perpendicular to the long external walls. The bracing walls should be distributed evenly along the length of the building.

2. Overturning forces

The racking forces shown in figure 49 also act to overturn the wall. This overturning must be resisted by providing a suitable tension member at each end of the wall. The member must transfer the forces to the substructure.

There are two common ways of providing this tension member in practice. One is to bolt the bottom wall plate to the subfloor and then provide structural joints between studs and plates to allow the force transfer. The other is to use a steel M12 threaded rod (anchor rod) extending from the top plate to the subfloor. Bracing walls will not work unless this overturning resistance is provided.

3. Bracing walls

Diagonal bracing

The need to provide bracing panels in framed engineering structures is well recognized. The usual method for steel-framed buildings is to provide diagonal cross-bracing. This method is used for both multi-storey buildings and low-rise buildings.

A similar method is followed in timber-framed house construction. A diagonal timber brace is often notched into the studs to keep the frame square. This practice may be suitable for low wind regions, although the strength of the system relies solely upon the adequacy of the fastening detail joining brace to plates. The following example shows the calculated strength of a diagonal bracing system.

Assume that the brace is set into the wall at an angle of 45° and is fastened to the top and bottom plate by two 75 x 3.75 mm nails at each end. Using unseasoned J3 hardwood, the basic lateral load per nail is 450 N [10, table 4.2.1.1]. Thus, the design strength of the diagonal to resist wind forces is 2 x 0.45 x 1.75 kN, or 1.6 kN.

The horizontal component of this force is 1.1 kN, which is very much less than the calculated racking force. Therefore diagonal bracing cannot be considered a suitable solution, as more than 20 such braces would be needed to resist the 23.2 kN racking force. (In practice, the brace would be nailed to the intermediate studs, which would contribute further to its strength, but would probably not increase it by 100 per cent.)

Diaphragm bracing

A more efficient method of providing bracing resistance against racking forces is the use of diaphragm action. In domestic timber construction, diaphragm bracing can be achieved by securely fastening a sheet cladding material to the wall to be braced. The sheet material may be plywood, hardboard, particle board, plaster board, asbestos cement or any other similar cladding material used for internal or external lining.

The racking strength of a bracing wall is dependent upon a number of parameters: length, width, sheet material properties, timber properties, nail size and spacing and overturning resistance. Walker [18] outlines a theoretical analysis of diaphragm bracing walls and derives the following formula for the bracing strength of a wall:

$$B = \frac{CF}{S} \qquad (4)$$

where

$$C = \frac{w(w + h)}{\sqrt{w^2 + h^2}} \ [1 - 2/3 \ \frac{wh}{(w^2 + h^2)}]$$

and w is the width of the wall, h is the height of the wall, F is the maximum force per fastener and S is the spacing of the fasteners.

The value of F must be empirically determined to suit the conditions in practice. It relates the timber properties, sheet properties and nail size. Some typical values of F are given by Walker. His formula applies only when the sheet material is not required to resist overturning forces, that is, when anchor rods are used.

A number of sheet cladding manufacturers have published brochures containing recommendations for the use of their material as a bracing wall. The recommendations are based on results of wall testing programmes rather than on theoretical analysis.

In the example given in section D.1, a racking force of 23.2 kN was calculated. The total length of plywood bracing walls needed to resist this force will now be calculated.

According to the design manual of the Plywood Association of Australia [19], a wall constructed as shown in figure 50 has a racking resistance of 4 kN per metre. Thus, the total length of wall required is 23.2/4, or 5.8 m.

Figure 50. Plywood bracing wall

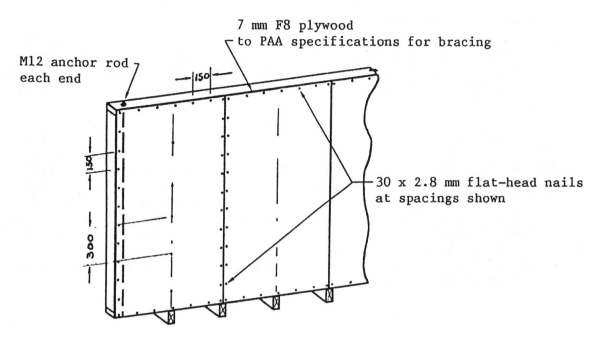

7 mm F8 plywood
to PAA specifications for bracing

M12 anchor rod
each end

150

150

300

30 x 2.8 mm flat-head nails
at spacings shown

As the studs are spaced at 450 mm, use plywood 900 mm wide. To distribute
the bracing walls evenly, locate a 900 mm length in two corners and two lengths
of approximately 2.0 m on internal walls spaced evenly along the length of the
house. Figure 51 shows this layout.

Figure 51. Location of bracing walls

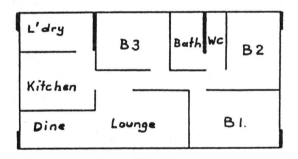

— denotes bracing wall

From a practical point of view, it would be easier to locate all the plywood bracing in the corners of the building, where it can be positioned in the
cavity of the brick veneer construction. However, that would result in a 14 m
length of wall between bracing walls, which is not structurally satisfactory.
Thus two internal walls were chosen to be bracing walls also, thereby reducing
the maximum length of wall between bracing walls to about 6 m.

4. Racking and uplift

In some instances, walls designated as bracing walls may also be used to
support and hold down the roof structure. During a wind storm, such walls
would be required to resist uplift forces as well as racking forces. The combination of these forces should be taken into account when designing bracing
walls.

5. <u>Ceiling diaphragms</u>

While it is readily accepted that external walls need to be braced by transverse internal walls, the role of the ceiling diaphragm is often over-looked. The diaphragm action at roof level is needed to transfer the racking forces from the top of the external walls to the bracing walls. In achieving this, the ceiling diaphragm prevents the external walls from bending too much between bracing walls.

In normal domestic construction, the ceiling is not designed to act as a diaphragm. As necessary as it is, any action of this kind is somewhat for-tuitous. Most sheet ceilings are able to offer some form of load transfer as a diaphragm, but their capacity to do so is very dependent on the fixings of ceiling material to battens and battens to ceiling joists [20]. As a result of an extensive test programme, Walker, Boughton and Gonano [21] have produced some interim design charts for ceiling diaphragms, for given sets of para-meters. These charts show that ceilings have the capacity to act as bracing diaphragms, even in cyclone-prone areas, when they are designed to do so. Figure 52 shows one such chart.

Figure 52. Design chart for W42 houses

Maximum shear wall spacing (m)

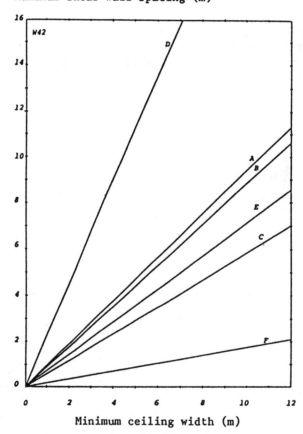

Minimum ceiling width (m)

Key: A. Gyprock and Versilux direct to joists as per tests 13 and 5, respectively
B. Versilux on timber battens as per test 6
C. Gyprock on timber battens as per test 15
D. Versilux on timber battens and nogging as per test 7
E. Gyprock on Lysaght battens as per test 12
F. Gyprock on furring channels as per test 3

Source: G. R. Walker, G. N. Boughton and D. Gonano, "Investigation of diaphragm action of ceilings: progress report 2", Technical Report No. 15, James Cook Cyclone Structural Testing Station, December 1982.

In order for both the bracing walls and ceiling diaphragm to act as structural systems, they must be connected by joints capable of transferring the racking force from the ceiling system to the bracing walls.

6. Roof diaphragms

Some roof claddings can also act as diaphragms to transfer forces from the external walls through the roof structure to internal bracing walls.

Ribbed or corrugated roof sheeting has the capacity to act as a diaphragm member, whereas discrete element systems such as roof tiles or shingles would probably have little such capacity.

Roof diaphragms have some disadvantages compared with ceiling diaphragms, but their capacity to transfer force through individual fasteners may be up to three times that of ceiling membranes. The obvious disadvantage is that the roof is pitched, so the sheeting is not in the same plane as the applied force. This also introduces a concern for the discontinuity of roof diaphragms at the ridge.

Another disadvantage of roof membranes is the discontinuity at adjacent sheets, although this can be overcome to some extent by using side lap fasteners between the roofing battens. However, side lap fasteners are rarely used in Australia.

The practice of fastening corrugated or ribbed sheeting through the crests reduces the effectiveness of the fasteners in transferring lateral forces: it requires the fasteners to act as cantilevers, an inefficient force transfer system.

Despite all these disadvantages, roof sheeting can be used as diaphragm bracing. Nash and Boughton [22] show that the following formula can be used to determine the onset of failure of 0.48 mm corrugated steel roof sheeting fastened with No. 12 screws into timber battens. The formula relates to loads on the building acting parallel to the corrugations:

$$W = \frac{2.6 \ nF}{b} \qquad (5)$$

where W is the uniformly distributed load at the top plate that gives rise to the onset of tearing in the roof sheeting, n is the number of battens in the stressed section of the roof, F is the tearing load of a single fastener loaded parallel to the corrugation and b is the length of the building measured perpendicular to the corrugations.

It should be noted that W in the above formula is not the design load but the force at which the sheet tears. A load factor still needs to be applied to determine the design load.

Care should be taken when using equation (5) as it makes no allowance for uplift forces acting on the roof sheeting. While this limitation may have little effect on the performance of a roofing membrane designed for non-cyclone conditions, it may seriously affect performance under the cyclic loading action of a cyclone.

E. Summary

Timber is a very suitable material to use in the construction of wind-resistant buildings, mainly because of its ability to resist frequent short-duration loading without fatigue. However, considerable attention must be given to the joints, as they are the potential weak links of the system. Racking forces can be resisted by traditional cladding materials engineered to form bracing walls and ceiling diaphragms.

References

1. G. R. Walker, "Report on cyclone Tracy – effect on buildings – December 1974" (Melbourne, Australian Department of Housing and Construction, 1975).

2. G. F. Reardon and R. M. Aynsley, "Houses to resist cyclone winds", Information Bulletin No. 1 (Townsville, Queensland, Australia, James Cook University Cyclone Testing Station, August 1979).

3. Timber Research and Development Advisory Council, Queensland Timber Framing Manual – W42 (Newstead, Queensland, Australia, 1979).

4. Timber Research and Development Advisory Council, Queensland Timber Framing Manual – W33 (Newstead, Queensland, Australia, 1979).

5. P. R. Smith and R.H.T. Adams, Domestic Construction Manual (Brisbane, Queensland, Australia, Master Builders Association, Department of Civil Engineering, Q.I.T., 1980).

6. K. J. Eaton, "Buildings and tropical windstorms", Overseas Building Note No. 188 (Watford, Herts., England, Building Research Establishment, April 1981).

7. Standards Association of Australia, Australian Standard 1170 Part 2-1981: SAA Loading Code, Part 2 – Wind Forces (Sydney, 1981).

8. G. F. Reardon and J. D. Holmes, "Wind tunnel tests on low rise buildings", Technical Report No. 11 (Townsville, Queensland, Australia, James Cook University Cyclone Testing Station, December 1981).

9. J. D. Holmes, "Mean and fluctuating internal pressures induced by wind", Proceedings of 5th International Conference on Wind Engineering (Fort Collins, Pergamon Press, 1979).

10. Standards Association of Australia, Australian Standard 1720-1975: SAA Timber Engineering Code (Sydney, 1975).

11. Standards Association of Australia, Australian Standard 1170 Part 1-1979: SAA Loading Code, Part 1 – Dead and Live Loads (Sydney, 1979).

12. G. F. Reardon, "The strength of batten-to-rafter joints. Part 2, recommendations for high wind areas", Technical Report No. 3 (Townsville, Queensland, Australia, James Cook University Cyclone Testing Station, March 1979).

13. Timber Engineering Co. Pty. Ltd., 1982 Catalogue and Specifications.

14. R. H. Leicester, Trends in Timber Engineering Research (Melbourne, CSIRO, Division of Building Research, 1978).

15. J. W. Morgan and V. R. Beck, "Sheet metal roof failures by repeated loading", Technical Report No. 2 (Melbourne, Australian Department of Housing and Construction, Housing Research Branch, July 1975).

16. V. R. Beck and J. W Morgan, "Appraisal of metal roofing under repeated wind loading - cyclone Tracy Darwin 1974", Technical Report No. 1 (Melbourne, Australian Department of Housing and Construction, Housing Research Branch, February 1975).

17. Experimental Building Station, "Guidelines for the testing and evaluation of products for cyclone-prone areas", Technical Record 440 (Department of Construction, February 1978).

18. G. R. Walker, "Racking strength of sheet clad wall panels", Proceedings of Diamond Jubilee Conference (Barton, Canberra, Australia, Institution of Engineers, April 1979).

19. Plywood Association of Australia, Structural Plywood Wall Bracing - Design Manual (Newstead, Queensland, August 1982).

20. G. R. Walker and D. Gonano, "Investigation of diaphragm action of ceilings - progress report 1", Technical Report No. 10 (Townsville, Queensland, Australia, James Cook University Cyclone Testing Station, November 1981).

21. G. R. Walker, G. N. Boughton and D. Gonano, "Investigation of diaphragm action of ceilings - progress report 2", Technical Report No. 15 (Townsville, Queensland, Australia, James Cook University Cyclone Testing Station, December 1982).

22. L. M. Nash, and G. N. Boughton, "Bracing strength of corrugated steel roofing", Technical Report No. 8 (Townsville, Queensland, Australia, James Cook University Cyclone Testing Station, September 1981).

VII. EARTHQUAKE RESISTANCE OF TIMBER BUILDINGS

G. B. Walford*

Introduction

Timber structures have the reputation of performing very well during earthquakes. This reputation may not be entirely fair since it is based largely on the performance of domestic buildings, which are not generally subject to engineering design. Accordingly, it probably results more from the inherent advantages of timber frame construction rather than from a conscious effort to provide earthquake resistance.

Knowledge gained from studies of the damage caused by earthquakes such as those that occurred in San Francisco in 1906, Tokyo in 1923, Anchorage in 1964 and many others has led to some understanding of the nature of earthquakes, their effects on buildings and how to provide earthquake resistance. A particularly good text book on this subject is Earthquake Resistant Design by Dowrick [1].

A. Earthquakes

Earthquakes are thought to arise from volcanic or tectonic (i.e. rock faulting) disturbances in the earth's crust. They produce vibrations in both the horizontal and vertical directions, but usually only the horizontal motion is considered in design, because the structure will be designed for vertical loading in any case. Maximum ground accelerations of 0.33 g were recorded in the El Centro earthquake of 1940, 0.5 g at Parkfield (1966) and as high as 1.17 g on a ridge near the Pocoima Dam, California (1971). No doubt earthquakes giving greater accelerations have occurred but were not recorded.

The recorded ground acceleration, together with the calculated distance from the hypocentre, or source, is used to calculate the magnitude M on the Richter scale from:

$$a = (1,080 \ e^{0.5M})/[(R + 25)^{1.32}]$$

where a is the peak acceleration in cm/s^2 and R is the distance from the source in km.

The largest earthquake ever recorded was the great Chilean earthquake of 1961, at M = 8.9. The Anchorage earthquake of 1964 was not much smaller, at M = 8.6. A shallow earthquake of, say, magnitude 6.5 and 5 km deep would cause serious damage, producing ground accelerations of about 0.32 g, whereas the same earthquake 250 km deep would hardly be noticed. Local geological features have a modifying effect. For instance, the observed shaking on soft ground may be twice as strong as that on solid rock and the shaking on a ridge may be twice as strong as that on level ground.

---

*Scientist, Forest Research Institute, Rotorua, New Zealand.

B. Building response

The response of a building to the ground motion depends on its natural frequency of vibration: if this is similar to the predominant frequencies in the ground motion and if the building has a typical viscous damping of 5 per cent, the ground motion can be amplified three or four times, owing to resonance effects. Therefore, in a severe earthquake with ground accelerations of 0.3 g, the elastic response of the building, or of parts of the building, such as the roof, may produce accelerations of 1.0 g or more. This amplification can be envisaged as a whiplash effect. In designing buildings to resist earthquakes, however, it is not expected that they should do so without damage, i.e. elastically, which implies that energy absorption will occur and the building response will be reduced.

The approach taken in design codes such as New Zealand Standard 4203:1976 [2] is that a building should resist a moderate earthquake, i.e. one up to about 0.20 g, without damage; stronger earthquakes, although causing damage, should not collapse the building. This philosophy means that there is an emphasis in aseismic design on ductility, the continuity of the building and the avoidance of collapse mechanisms.

C. Timber buildings in earthquakes

From the report of Cooney [3] on the observed performance of timber houses in New Zealand during earthquakes, it appears that timber-framed houses are inherently ductile, but conscious effort must be made to provide continuity and to avoid collapse mechanisms. He concludes as follows: "The traditional New Zealand house constructed of light timber framing, clad with weatherboards, having moderate window openings, and having a steel roof is a sound earthquake resistant structure. However it is often founded on inadequate foundations." Typically, these inadequate foundations were unbraced pile systems, as shown in figure 53 or basement garages with large openings in one wall.

Figure 53. Unbraced pile system supporting a timber-framed house

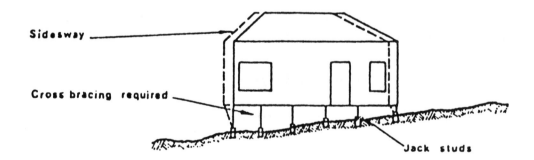

Dowrick [1] identifies the following causes of inadequate performance of timber construction in earthquakes:

(a) Large response on soft ground;

(b) Lack of integrity of substructure;

(c) Asymmetry of the structural form (e.g. basement garages);

(d) Insufficient strength of chimneys (sometimes no reinforcement, with brick chimneys being particularly poor);

(e) Inadequate structural connections (particularly between components of different stiffness as in masonry veneer construction);

(f) Use of heavy roofs without appropriate strength of supporting frame;

(g) Deterioration of timber through insect or fungal attack;

(h) Inadequate resistance to post-earthquake fires.

Williams [4] considers the advantages of timber construction to be as follows:

(a) Timber has a distinct advantage in that it can weigh as little as one tenth as much as concrete construction;

(b) Timber is usually several times less stiff than alternative forms of construction. This may be an advantage in that the period is lengthened and the response may be reduced. However, non-structural damage may be severe if deflections are large;

(c) The natural damping of wood is low, about 2 per cent, but because of the damping that occurs in the many connections in a timber structure, its equivalent viscous damping and peak response to earthquake vibrations compare favourably with those of other materials, as shown in table 11;

(d) Because of the natural variability of timber, design strength levels are lower, relative to mean ultimate strength, than for other materials, often giving a reserve of strength in load-sharing constructions;

(e) Timber in flexure is not ductile, but its connections frequently are;

(f) Mechanical connections in timber structures generally show good energy absorption under cyclic loading. The high energy absorption performance of nailed timber and plywood shear walls is shown in figure 54;

(g) Ease of repair and strengthening may be a reason why little earthquake damage in timber structures is reported. Any move to larger or heavier multi-storey timber buildings may mean this aspect should be reappraised.

Table 11. Equivalent viscous damping and relative response
for various structures
(Per cent)

Type of construction	Damping	Response
Steel frame, welded, all walls flexible	2	100
Steel frame, welded or bolted, stiff cladding, internal walls flexible	5	73
Steel frame, welded or bolted, with concrete shear walls	7	65
Concrete frame, all walls flexible	5	73
Concrete frame, stiff cladding, internal walls flexible	7	65
Concrete frame, with concrete or masonry shear walls	10	58
Concrete or masonry shear wall building	10	58
Timber shear wall or diaphragm construction	15	50

Source: D. J. Dowrick, Earthquake Resistant Design (New York, John Wiley and Sons, 1977).

Figure 54. Hysteretic behaviour of timber diaphragms under
cyclic loading

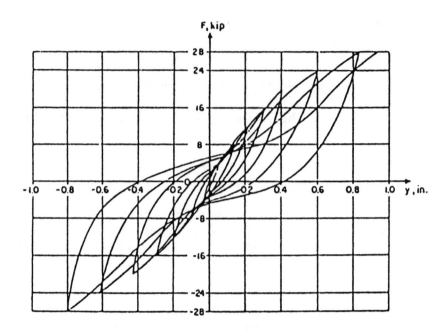

Source: K. Medearis, "Static and dynamic properties of shear
structures", Proceedings of the International Symposium on the Effects of
Repeated Loadings on Materials and Structures, RILEM, Mexico, 1966.

D. Design forces

NZS 4203 [2] gives design accelerations of between 0.1 and 0.36 g for
timber buildings, depending on factors such as site seismicity, soil flexibil-
ity, building period, building ductility, importance and risk. Assuming that:

(a) Roof and wall dead load = 0.25 kPa (5 psf);

(b) Floor dead plus live load = 1.25 kPa (25 psf);

(c) Storey height = 3 m (10 ft);

(d) Building is rectangular with H/B < 5 and D/B $\cong$ 1;

(e) Seismic coefficient = c.

The total equivalent lateral load E on a building can be calculated, in
kN, using the following relationship:

$$E = c \left\{ BD[0.25 + 1.25(N - 1)] + 2H(B + D)0.25 \right\}$$

where N is the number of storeys.

This result should be compared to the design wind force required by
NZS 4203, because wind frequently governs for single-storey timber buildings.
Assuming that:

(a) Maximum 3-sec gust speed expected in 50 yr = V, in m/sec;

(b) Topography factor S_1 = 1.0;

(c) Ground roughness = 3 (i.e. well-wooded areas, towns and cities);

(d) Building size = class B (not greater than 50 m);

(e) Roughness/class/size factor S_2 related to height H by

S_2	H						
	3	5	10	15	20	30	40
	0.60	0.65	0.74	0.83	0.90	0.97	1.01

(f) Pressure coefficient = 1.2.

The total lateral wind force W may be calculated using the following relationship:

$$W = 1.2 \ HB \times 0.613(S_1 S_2 V)^2 N$$

Figures 55 and 56, obtained by equating E and W, show the situations where wind or earthquake govern the design for lateral load on, respectively, single-storey buildings and two-storey buildings. These figures show that in areas prone to tropical cyclones, i.e. winds in excess of 50 m/sec (112 mph), in single-storey buildings wind loading will usually govern while in two-storey buildings more than 12 m deep, earthquake may be critical.

Figure 55. Correspondence between wind speed and earthquake
forces on single-storey timber buildings

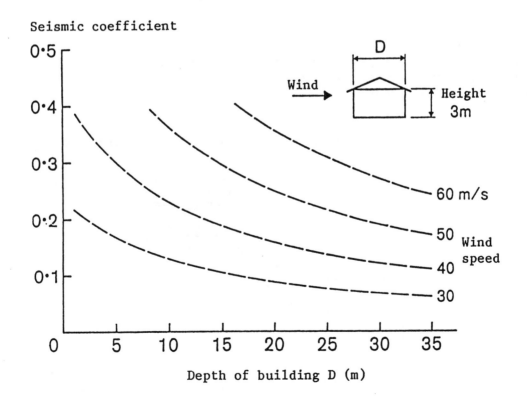

Figure 56. Correspondence between wind speed and earthquake forces
on two-storey timber buildings

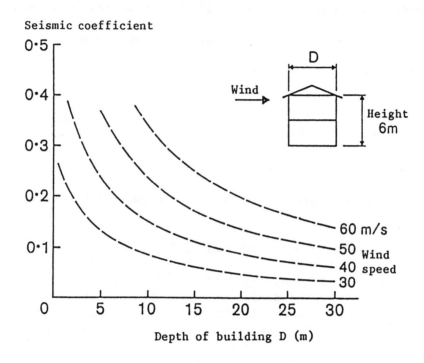

E. <u>Design details</u>

There follow brief comments on types of timber construction that are described in detail in other chapters.

1. <u>Poles</u>

Pole frame and pole platform construction (figure 57) provide particularly good earthquake resistance provided effective connections are made to the poles and their ground embedment is sufficient.

Figure 57. Pole frame and pole platform construction

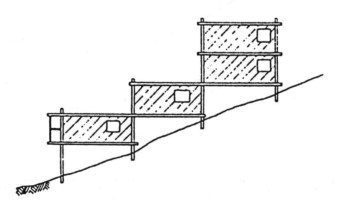

2. <u>Moment-resisting frames</u>

Nailed, pre-drilled steel plate, galvanized or otherwise protected against corrosion, makes a very effective moment-resisting joint between large rectangular timber members (figure 58). Portal frames and two-storey frames have been built in this system in New Zealand. The joint can be designed to yield in the nail-to-timber connection, in which case it possesses good ductility. The joint is by no means novel, being a large version of the common Gang-Nail plate or a development of the glulam rivet used in Canada but applied to moment-resisting joints rather than resisting axial loads.

Figure 58. Moment-resisting frame and joint detail

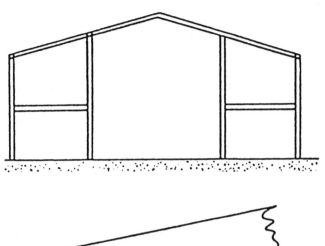

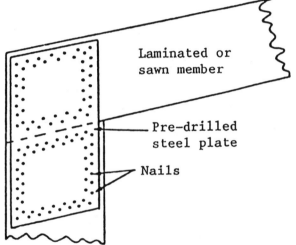

A similar concept is the use of nailed plywood gussets, particularly suited to portal frames (figure 59). These have been tested recently by Batchelar [5], verifying the results of McKay [6].

Figure 59. Nailed plywood gusset

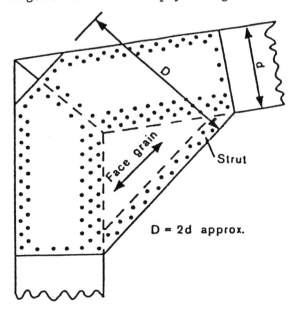

3. Shear walls and diaphragms

Panel materials such as plywood are used to resist shear loads in wall, roof and floor diaphragms (figure 60) and box beams. The American Institute of Timber Construction [7] gives details of design methods. Figure 54 showed a typical load/deflection curve for a plywood-sheathed shear wall under racking loads. It should be emphasized that the ductile behaviour derives from deformations in the nailed connection between the panels and the framing and not in the panel or framing itself. Therefore it is possible to use a comparatively brittle panel material, such as asbestos cement.

Figure 60. Structure using shear walls and diaphragms

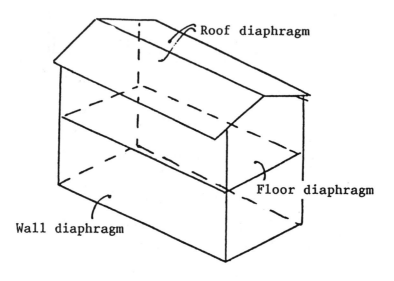

4. Diagonal bracing

Light timber frame houses are commonly braced within the walls using light metal braces of flat or angle cross section (figure 61). Like solid timber diagonal bracing these rely entirely on the fastening at each end for their effectiveness. Where walls are not lined with a panel material, these braces are essential, but tests have shown that sheet materials give several times greater rigidity than diagonal braces (figure 62).

Figure 61. Structure using diagonal braces

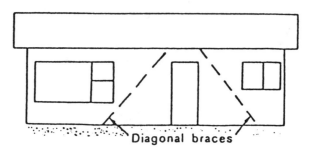

Figure 62. Diagonal bracing with sheet material

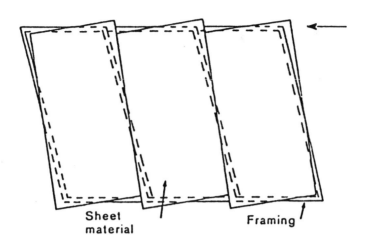

Sheet material   Framing

References

1. D. J. Dowrick, <u>Earthquake Resistant Design</u> (New York, John Wiley and Sons, 1977).

2. Standards Association of New Zealand, <u>General Structural Design and Design Loadings for Buildings: NZS 4203</u> (Wellington, 1976).

3. R. C. Cooney, "The structural performance of houses in earthquakes", Reprint No. 13 (Wellington, Building Research Association of New Zealand, 1979).

4. R. L. Williams, "Timber and earthquake engineering", New Zealand Timber Design Society Newsletter No. 9 (1982).

5. M. L. Batchelar, "Plywood gusset joints for timber portals", New Zealand Timber Design Society Newsletter No. 11 (1983).

6. D. McKay, "Investigation of plywood gussets in timber portal frames", Project Report (Parkhurst, Queensland, Australia, Capricornia Institute of Advanced Education).

7. American Institute of Timber Construction, <u>Timber Construction Manual</u> (New York, John Wiley and Sons, 1986).

VIII. LOAD TESTING OF STRUCTURES

Robert H. Leicester*

Introduction

Load tests are undertaken for several reasons, and it is important in any particular load test that the exact purpose of the test is clear. This is often not the case, and many load-testing specifications are unsatisfactory for their intended purpose. In addition, difficulties are encountered in assessing composite constructions because of differences in test specifications for structures of different materials. This report is intended to clarify the conceptual aspects of load testing. Only a brief mention will be made of practial considerations.

Most load tests can be considered to have, broadly, one of three purposes:

(a) To obtain the acceptance of a structure for a specific purpose;

(b) To obtain information to assist in the assessment of a structure;

(c) To provide a method of quality control in the construction of structures.

In a load test specification it is important to define the structural state that is being assessed. In general this will be either an ultimate limit state or a serviceability limit state:

(a) Ultimate limit states are states in which a structure is rendered unfit for further use. Typically, ultimate limit states follow the attainment of maximum load capacity. Usually it is desirable that there is only a small risk that a structure reach an ultimate limit state during its design lifetime;

(b) Serviceability limit states are states in which a structure fails to perform satisfactorily but is still fit for further use. Examples of this are excessive deflections, vibrations and cracking. Often it is acceptable for a structure to reach its serviceability limit state a few times during it design lifetime.

A. Acceptance testing

There are three common types of acceptance load tests:

(a) Proof testing of an existing structure;

(b) Proof testing of every new structure in a class;

(c) Prototype testing of a sample of structures in a class.

---

*An officer of CSIRO, Division of Building Research, Melbourne.

A generalized format for the loads to be used in these tests may be written as

$$L_{test} = K_C K_D K_U L_{design} \tag{1}$$

where L_{test} is a maximum load to be applied during the acceptance test, L_{design} is a design load specified for the structure under test, K_C is a factor to compensate for the differences between the test and in-service loading and structural configurations, K_D is a factor to compensate for the differences between the test and in-service load duration effects and K_U is a factor to cover uncertainties of the in-service loads and strengths.

The basic concepts of the three methods of acceptance testing mentioned above will be described next and the various aspects of acceptance testing will be briefly commented on. A method for deriving load factors to be used in acceptance testing is described in annex I.

1. Proof testing of existing structures

General

There are many reasons for requiring that an existing structure be tested. These include a doubt that the structure has the specified design chracteristics because of errors in design or construction or because of deterioration since construction, such as can result from fire, chemical attack or material degradation. It also often happens that a structure is to be put to a new use for which it was not originally designed but for which it nevertheless may have an adequate structural capacity. In this case, a proof test may be used to demonstrate that the structure has the necessary capacity.

Ultimate limit states

As indicated in annex I, a typical test load for checking the ultimate limit states of structures or structural elements with respect to the loads specified in AS 1170 [1], [2] is as follows:

$$L_{test} = K_C K_D (1.2 \, L_D + 1.3 \, L_W + 1.3 \, L_L) \tag{2}$$

where L_D, L_W and L_L are the specified design loads in AS 1170 for dead, wind and floor live loads, respectively. The factors 1.2 and 1.3 in equation (2) may be interpreted as factors of safety to allow for the possibility that the specified design loads may be exceeded during the lifetime of the structure.

For a proof test on an existing structure to be successful, it is necessary not only that the structure does not reach its ultimate limit state during the test but also that it does not incur serious permanent structural damage. Suitable methods for detecting the onset of damage vary from one material to another and include such techniques as the measurement of crack width and acoustic emissions. One commonly used method is the measurement of recovery of the deformation when the structure is unloaded after the test. Table 12 shows the recovery values recommended by CSN 732030, the Czechoslovak State Standard, and reported in [3]. Finally, a comment should be made on often-expressed opinion that damage to a structure can be avoided by using a sufficiently small test load. Since an existing structure is usually proof-tested because its strength is unknown, there would appear to be no way of specifying a test load (solely in terms of a load factor) that could be guaranteed not to damage the structure.

Table 12. Required recovery of deformation after
proof testing

Structural material	Recovery (%)
Steel	85
Pre-stressed concrete	80
Reinforced concrete, masonry	75
Timber	70
Plastic	70

Source: R. Bares and N. Fitzsimons, "Load tests of building structures", American Society of Civil Engineers: Structural Division: Journal, vol. 101, No. ST5, Proceedings Paper 11322 (May 1975), pp. 1111-1123.

Serviceability limit states

As indicated in annex I, a typical test load for checking serviceability limit states with respect to the loads specified in AS 1170 is as follows:

$$L_{test} = K_C K_D (L_D + 0.7 \ L_W + 0.6 \ L_L) \qquad (3)$$

This is a smaller test load than the one specified in equation (2) for testing ultimate limit states, because the consequences of reaching the serviceability limit state are considerably less than those of reaching the ultimate limit state.

2. Proof testing applied to every new structure

The proof testing of every structural unit is sometimes the basis of acceptance for a class of structures or structural elements. Examples of this include pressure vessels and high-pressure gas pipelines [4]. Proof testing has also been proposed as a method of grading structural timber [5].

In proof tests of this type, proof loads similar to those specified in equations (2) and (3) for assessing existing structures may be used. However for this case, a target strength for the structural units must also be speci-fied. Ideally this would be taken as the cost-optimized value given in annex I. However, if the possibility exists that the structural unit may be damaged by proof testing, then either the target strength must be made sufficiently high that the proof test does not cause damage or the proof load must be inc-reased to compensate for the possible loss in strength due to proof testing. An example of this latter method has been described by Leicester [5].

3. Prototype testing

In the application of prototype tests, the acceptance of a complete class of structures is based on the structural performance of a sample of these structures. The sample size is often quite small, and a sample comprising a single structural unit is not uncommon. In these tests, structural units are usually, but not necessarily, loaded to failure. Many methods are used for interpreting the observations during the test. These vary not only from one type of structural unit to another but also with the type of test results obtained. The following describes simple criteria that are convenient to use in test specifications. The derivation of these criteria is discussed in annex I.

Ultimate limit states

For structural units intended to carry the loads considered in AS 1170, the acceptance criterion is that all structures in a sample of size N demonstrate their ability to sustain the following load without reaching their ultimate limite states:

$$L_{test} = K_C K_D K_U (L_D + L_W + L_L) \qquad (4)$$

where the appropriate uncertainty parameter K_U is given in table 13. This parameter is intended to cover the possibility that the in-service loads may exceed the load specified in AS 1170 and also the fact that the structural units of the sample may be stronger than average.

Table 13. The uncertainty factor K_U for prototype
testing of ultimate limit states

Coefficient of variation of strength	Typical structural element	K_U a/		
		N = 1	N = 2	N = 5
0.1	Nailed joint	2.0	1.9	1.8
0.2	Compression strength of timber	3.6	3.2	2.8
0.3	Bending strength of timber	6.6	5.5	4.3

a/ N is sample size.

It is to be noted from table 13 that there is a large increase in the required load factor with the increase in variability of the structural units. To some extent the need for these large load factors may be reduced by the use of selective sampling techniques. For example, in the prototype testing of timber structures, a considerable reduction in the required load factor can often be obtained by specifying that all timber used in the fabrication of the test structures shall be of the lowest structural quality that is acceptable for the specified structural timber grades used.

Serviceability limit states

For structural units intended to sustain the loads considered in AS 1170, the acceptance criterion is that the average load at which the serviceability limit state is reached is not greater than the following:

$$L_{test} = K_C K_D (1.1\ L_D + 0.8\ L_W + 0.7\ L_L) \qquad (5)$$

This load is only slightly larger than that specified in equation (3) for proof testing. This is because the load factor necessary to cover the variability of structural response is to a large extent taken into account by the load factors included in both cases to cover the uncertainties of the in-service loads and user response.

4. Configuration load factor K_C

Factor for incorrect structural modelling

Often in acceptance testing, particularly in prototype testing, only a portion of the complete in-service structure is available or active during a load test, and the specified test load may need to be modified to compensate for this. Typical examples of incorrect modelling frequently occur with buckling restraints and load-sharing mechanisms.

Factor for incorrect load modelling

Test loads are usually very idealized representations of true in-service loads. Distributed loads are usually approximated by strip or point loads, and stochastic loads are represented in tests either by simplified stochastic loads or even by static loads, as is done in AS 1170 for wind loads and floor live loads. In all cases it is necessary to exercise considerable care in choosing the load factor K_C to ensure that the correct structural effect is obtained. Some discussion on this is given in annex II, where it is shown that the factor K_C depends not only on the characteristics of the load but also on the characteristics of the structural response.

5. Duration load factor K_D

The duration load factor K_D compensates for differences of structural response to short-term test loads and long-term, in-service loads. These differences may arise due to changes in strength of structural material with time. For example, normal concrete will increase in strength with time, whereas high-alumina-cement concrete can decrease in strength. Also, the strength of some materials, such as timber, plastics and glass, is sensitive to the duration of load application. Finally, there are the effects of creep, which change not only deformations but also the buckling strength of slender structural elements. As an example of the duration load factor, annex III shows some values that are recommended for timber structures.

6. Difficulties in the use of load tests as a basis for acceptance

Attention has already been paid to some of the difficulties encountered in the use of load tests as a basis for the acceptance of a structure. There is the danger of causing damage, and there are problems with choosing the correct load factors K_C, K_D and K_U. Often these difficulties cannot be overcome completely, even in concept, because to do so would require a detailed prior knowledge of the characteristics of the structure to be tested.

Another serious difficulty arises from the fact that most load tests are made on multiple member and/or composite structures. For this situation, the load factors K_U and K_D can differ considerably from one element to another. Testing specifications usually require that the composite load factor $K_U K_D$ should be the largest one noted when the structure is considered on an element-by-element basis. One method to avoid this conservative approach is to carefully reinforce a structure so that failure occurs at the location where uncertainty exists; the remainder of the structure is then assessed solely on the basis of design computations. Obviously, the reinforcement must be done in such a way that it does not affect the stresses in the critical location of interest.

Of more serious consequence in multiple-member and composite structures is the fact that differences in variability and long duration characteristics of the various elements imply that in a load test the typical mode of failure may be quite different from that of the weakest 5 per cent of the population, or quite different from that of structures in service over a long period of time. There would appear to be no general method of overcoming this deficiency when the acceptance of a structure is based solely on load tests.

7. Comparison between acceptance procedures

Two types of load test procedures for the acceptance of structures have been described, namely the proof and prototype test methods. In addition to these, the acceptance of structures may be obtained from several other procedures including that of design, which is probably the most common procedure. It should be apparent that the information used to make an assessment differs from one method to another, so the actual assessment of particular structures will also differ, depending on which method has been used.

Methods for design computations are usually based on extensive data and experience and as a result are associated with moderate load factors to allow for the uncertainties of in-service loads and strength. In prototype tests, most of the uncertainties related to structural theory are eliminated, but unless the structural material is of low variability, assessments based on these tests carry a heavy load factor penalty due to the possibility that the test sample may contain unusually strong structures. By contrast, structures that survive a proof test have almost no uncertainties concerning their guaranteed strength, and the small required load factor covers the possibility that the real load exceeds L_{design}. Thus it may be stated that, in general terms, the use of prototype testing is most effective for use with structures having a low variability and proof testing is most effective for structures having a high variability.

8. Practical considerations

Information on practical aspects of load testing have been given in papers by Bares and Fitzsimons [3], Menzies [6], and Jones and Oliver [7]. The following is intended to highlight some general points that need to be considered in embarking on a load testing programme.

Specifications

It is difficult, in fact probably impossible, to write a set of specifications that is applicable for load testing all types of structures. However, there is a strong incentive to make the specifications as tight as possible so as to minimize conflicts between the various parties involved in a load-testing operation.

Apart from the specification of a test load, it is important to be specific when defining the ultimate and serviceability limit states. Usually, the ultimate limit state is defined as the loss of structural integrity, but there are times when it may be convenient to define it in terms of excessive cracking or deformation. The latter definition is often useful for structural elements that fail through buckling. In the specification of serviceability limit states, it is important to ensure that realistic, rather than the traditional nominal, values of limit states are used. For example, it is common to specify that the computed nominal deflection of a beam be limited to 0.002 of the span, whereas it is well known that a deflection of 0.0001 of the span can crack brittle masonry walls.

Other aspects that should be mentioned in a test load specification include the method of sampling to be used for choosing the test structures in prototype testing, the required accuracy of load and deformation measurements, the conditions for permitting the local reinforcing of parts of a structure that are not under test and the conditions for permitting a retest should a structure or set of structures fail a load test.

Important structures

A reduced risk of failure is required for important structures such as those that have to operate in post-disaster situations. The necessary increase in load factors for such structures is contained in the method used for the derivation of load factors described in annex I. However, it should be noted that to obtain low probabilities of failure in practice, it is necessary not only to have an appropriate margin of safety but also to ensure that the probability of occurrence of a human error is considerably reduced from its normal value [8].

Load factors for rare loads

Some load events, such as domestic gas explosions, have a small but real chance of occurrence on any one particular structure. A method of deriving suitable load factors for this is given in annex I.

Safety during a load test

Large loads are usually employed during a load test, and precautions must be taken to ensure that if the test unit fails no damage is done to other, related structures or to personnel. Failures during load tests are usually dangerous when the failure mode is brittle and are also dangerous when the loading is carried out by the application of dead weights.

B. Load tests to obtain information

In view of the difficulties associated with the acceptance of a structure solely on the basis of a load test, it is frequently more useful to use a load test to provide information to remedy a gap in structural theory. There are four ways in which this information can be used.

1. Indication of failure modes

A load test can be very useful in indicating modes of failure that may not have been considered in a design process. Once the failure mode is determined, a simple design theory can be derived to fit the test information. However, some caution is advised in the application of this procedure, because as mentioned earlier, the choice of a correct type of load depends to some extent on a prior knowledge of the critical structural response.

2. Strength of a failure mode

A load test may be used to measure the strength of a failure mode that is difficult to analyse. Examples of such modes are the fracture of a complex joint and the buckling of a structure of complex geometry.

3. Check on expected behaviour

A third method of using load test information is to check the observed failure modes and the average test strength against the predictions of a theory or against information obtained from previous load tests.

A useful example of this would be in the assessment of a new type of timber truss. In such a case the use of conventional prototype test procedures would be extremely conservative because of the great variability of some of the structural elements concerned; they would also be difficult to apply because of the great differences between the variability and duration effects of the various members and connectors and because of the uncertainty of the correct buckling restraints that occur in real structural situations. However, past experience of load tests on various types of trusses that have proven to be satisfactory in service has shown that in a standard laboratory load test, these trusses have, on average, a strength that is 3.7 times the design load and that the coefficient of variation between the mean strengths of different types of trusses is 15 per cent. On the basis of this information, a new type of timber truss could be considered to be satisfactory if its test strength, on average, is not less than one standard deviation from the overall mean value, i.e. if it is at least 3.1 times the design load.

4. Measurement of an index property

Load tests are frequently undertaken to measure a structural index property that is then used as a parameter in a design process. Since this technique is usually based on extensive research and experience relevant to specific design processes, a discussion of it is outside the scope of this chapter.

An example of this technique is the use of load tests for the design of foundations. Another example is the use of the standard tests specified in AS 1649-1974 [9] to obtain basic working loads for metal fasteners in timber; these derived design strengths are then applied in design according to the rules of AS 1720-1975, Timber Engineering Code [10].

C. Quality control

Load tests are frequently used as a form of quality control. Examples of such tests are cylinder tests on concrete and tests on samples of finger-jointed timber members taken at specified intervals from a production line. In all cases, it is important to appreciate that quality control does not in itself form an acceptance method. It requires a separate and frequently more important operation to demonstrate the connection between the performance of a structure and the results of quality control tests. Unfortunately, quality control specifications are often written on the basis of the quality that can be attained in a test, often specific to a particular laboratory or production line, and with very little regard for their relationship to the performance of the structure.

The function of quality control testing is essentially either to detect a gradual drift away from a target quality or to detect a sudden breakdown in a production process. Table 14 gives a rough estimate of the statistical properties of samples of size N. If any of these properties drift more than two standard deviations from their expected values, it is highly probable that there has been a change in the production process.

The four essential elements in the specification of quality control procedures are the following:

(a) The rate of sampling;

(b) The type of load test to be carried out;

(c) The criteria for deciding that action is to be taken;

(d) The nature of the action to be taken.

Table 14. Statistical properties of samples

Sample parameter	Approximate value for sample of size N a/	
	Mean or expected value	Standard deviation
Mean	X	$\sigma/\sqrt{N}$
Coefficient of variation	V	$V/\sqrt{2N}$
Coefficient of skewness	β	$\sqrt{6}/N$
Kurtosis	g	$24/N$

a/ X, σ, V, β and g are, respectively, the mean, standard deviation, coefficient of variation, coefficient of skewness and kurtosis of the parent population.

In deciding on the above, the following factors should be considered and preferably stated in an annex to each quality control specification:

(a) The relationship between the quality control test and the performance of the associated structures;

(b) The variability of the product assessed;

(c) The probable rate of change in the quality of the product;

(d) The effective cost of not taking corrective action when the criteria in the specification indicate that this should be done;

(e) The reaction time to adjust a production process and the consequences of this;

(f) The effect of the occasional severe undetected anomaly occurring in the production process.

On the basis of the above information, a quality control specification may be derived through a rational procedure rather than through an intuitive one, as is more usual. A simple illustrative example of this procedure is given in annex IV.

Finally, it should be noted that unless the proof testing of every production element is undertaken, quality control tests will not detect the occasional serious anomaly in quality. For example, if finger-jointed timber members are to be used in primary trusses, then their structural performance is critical and the proof testing of every member will be necessary to ensure the reliable structural performance of the trusses in which they are used.

D. <u>Summary</u>

The types of load test commonly undertaken have been grouped into three broad classifications related to the objectives of obtaining acceptance, information and quality control. For each of these classifications an attempt has been made to systematize the conceptual aspects of load testing. Only brief mention has been made of practical considerations.

Of the two types of acceptance load test described, the prototype test is particularly effective for removing the uncertainties of structural actions, but it is usually unacceptably conservative when applied to structures with high material variability. The proof test is useful in ensuring that a particular structure does not contain a serious structural defect. It is expensive to use in that it has to be applied to every structure under consideration, but it has the advantage that among the various approval systems discussed it requires the lowest load factor for acceptance. This is particularly useful for application to structural units that exhibit a considerable variability between nominally identical structures, because in such a case a large safety factor would be required in design.

In many practical situations, it is difficult to write a meaningful specification for acceptance load tests, because of the uncertainties of the statistical properties of loads and strengths, the uncertainties of long-term in-service effects and the complex actions of multiple-member and composite structures. Often, particularly when only limited load-testing can be undertaken, the most effective use of a load test is to provide information to fill an ignorance gap in the design process.

In the use of load tests as a quality control procedure, it is important to appreciate that the quality control tests do not in themselves form an approval system. In all cases it is necessary to demonstrate the relationship between the quality control tests and the properties of the related structure under consideration.

Annex I

LOAD FACTORS FOR ACCEPTANCE TESTING

A. Load factors for ultimate limit states

1. Method

One simple theory for the derivation of load factors has been described in previous papers by Leicester [5], [11], [12]. It is based on the optimization of the total costs, made up of the initial cost of the structure and the costs incurred if failures occur, either in service or during proof testing. In this theory, the uncertainties related to strength, denoted by R, and loads, denoted by S, are represented by two simple random variables, as shown in figure 63.

Figure 63. Distributions of load and strength

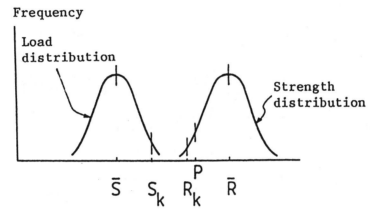

The magnitudes of R and S are indicated by their mean values $\bar{R}$ and $\bar{S}$ or by characteristic values R_k and S_k, which are typically defined by

$$R_k = R_{0.05} \qquad (1)$$

$$S_k = S_{0.90} \qquad (2)$$

where $R_{0.05}$ and $S_{0.90}$ are the five-percentile and ninety-percentile values of R and S, respectively. The uncertainties of R and S are indicated by their coefficients of variation, denoted by V_R and V_S, respectively. Typically, these coefficients range from 0.1 to 0.3.

Three cost parameters are used in the reliability theory. The first, denoted by α, is related to C_S, the cost of the structure, by

$$C_S = A\bar{R}^{\alpha} \qquad (3)$$

where A is a constant for a given type of structure. If it is assumed that cost is proportional to the volume of material used, then $\alpha = 1.0$ for tension members, $\alpha = 2/3$ for the bending strength of geometrically similar beams and $\alpha = 1/2$ for the bending strength of plates. The second cost parameter, denoted by C_{FSO}, is the relative cost incurred if failure occurs, and it is defined by

$$C_{FSO} = C_{FS}/C_{SO} \qquad (4)$$

where C_{FS} is the absolute effective cost if failure occurs and C_{SO} is the cost of the optimum structure. Typical values of C_{FSO} range from 10 to 1,000.

The third cost parameter, denoted by C_{FP}, is the cost incurred if failure occurs during proof testing.

Because there are usually inadequate data to make accurate assessments of the probabilities of failure associated with ultimate limit states, it is necessary to calibrate any theoretical model used to derive load factors. One method of doing this is to choose the input parameters so that the load factors derived for design computations agree with those currently used in structural codes and considered to be correct. Thus, for purposes of calibration, table 15 gives load factors for design. It should be noted that the appropriate relative cost of failure to be used in the derivation of load factors for design is often an order of magnitude greater than that used for test loads, because load tests often involve a complete assemblage of elements, whereas design decisions are usually concerned with single structural elements.

Table 15. Load factors for design

| | | | Load factor $K_U = R_{min}/S_{0.90}$ a/ | | | | | |
| | | | $C_{FSO} = 30$ | | | $C_{FSO} = 300$ | | |
V_R	V_S		N = 1	N = 2	N = 5	N = 1	N = 2	N = 5
0.50	0.1	0.1	1.61	1.52	1.41	1.94	1.83	1.70
		0.2	1.59	1.50	1.39	1.92	1.81	1.68
		0.3	1.64	1.55	1.44	1.98	1.87	1.74
	0.2	0.1	2.51	2.23	1.90	3.73	3.31	2.83
		0.2	2.38	2.11	1.80	3.53	3.14	2.67
		0.3	2.32	2.06	1.76	3.45	3.06	2.61
	0.3	0.1	3.89	3.23	2.52	7.23	6.00	4.69
		0.2	3.61	2.99	2.34	6.71	5.57	4.35
		0.3	3.43	2.84	2.22	6.37	5.28	4.13
0.75	0.1	0.1	1.55	1.47	1.36	1.88	1.77	1.64
		0.2	1.54	1.45	1.35	1.86	1.75	1.62
		0.3	1.59	1.50	1.39	1.92	1.81	1.68
	0.2	0.1	2.34	2.08	1.77	3.48	3.09	2.64
		0.2	2.22	1.97	1.68	3.30	2.92	2.50
		0.3	2.16	1.92	1.64	3.22	2.86	2.44
	0.3	0.1	3.49	2.89	2.26	6.50	5.38	4.20
		0.2	3.23	2.68	2.10	6.01	4.99	3.90
		0.3	3.07	2.55	1.99	5.71	4.74	3.70
1.00	0.1	0.1	1.52	1.43	1.33	1.83	1.73	1.61
		0.2	1.50	1.42	1.31	1.81	1.71	1.59
		0.3	1.55	1.46	1.36	1.87	1.77	1.64

continued

Table 15 (<u>continued</u>)

		Load factor $K_U = R_{min}/S_{0.90}$ a/					
		$C_{FSO} = 30$			$C_{FSO} = 300$		
V_R	V_S	$N = 1$	$N = 2$	$N = 5$	$N = 1$	$N = 2$	$N = 5$
0.2	0.1	2.26	1.98	1.69	3.31	2.94	2.51
	0.2	2.11	1.87	1.60	3.14	2.78	2.38
	0.3	2.06	1.83	1.56	3.06	2.72	2.32
0.3	0.1	3.23	2.68	2.09	6.00	4.98	3.89
	0.2	2.99	2.48	1.94	5.57	4.62	3.61
	0.3	2.84	2.36	1.84	5.28	4.38	3.42

a/ R_{min} = minimum strength in a sample of N structures.

2. Computed load factors

The load factors in tables 16–18 have been computed with assumed Weibull distributions for strengths and loads. The appropriate parameters of V_R, V_S, C_{FP} and C_{FSO} to be used are those that have been derived from a consideration of only those aspects that relate directly to the choice of load factor. For example, fixed costs are not to be included for consideration in the evaluation of α, C_{FP} and C_{FSO}.

Table 16. Load factors for the proof testing
of existing structures

	$K_U = P/S_{0.90}$ a/	
V_S	$C_{FS}/C_{FP} = 30$	$C_{FS}/C_{FP} = 300$
0.1	1.03	1.08
0.2	1.07	1.17
0.3	1.10	1.27

a/ P = proof load.

Table 17. Load factors for the proof testing of
every new structure

			Load factor			
			$K_U = P/S_{0.90}$ a/		$H = \bar{R}/S_{0.90}$ b/	
α	V_R	V_S	$C_{FSO} = 30$	$C_{FSO} = 300$	$C_{FSO} = 30$	$C_{FSO} = 300$
0.5	0.1	0.1	1.03	1.08	1.31	1.36
		0.2	1.07	1.17	1.40	1.50
		0.3	1.11	1.27	1.50	1.67

continued

Table 17 (<u>continued</u>)

		Load factor			
		$K_U = P/S_{0.90}$ a/		$H = \bar{R}/S_{0.90}$ b/	
V_R	V_S	$C_{FSO} = 30$	$C_{FSO} = 300$	$C_{FSO} = 30$	$C_{FSO} = 300$
0.2	0.1	1.03	1.08	1.49	1.54
	0.2	1.07	1.17	1.57	1.70
	0.3	1.10	1.27	1.68	1.88
0.3	0.1	1.03	1.08	1.63	1.69
	0.2	1.06	1.17	1.72	1.85
	0.3	1.10	1.27	1.83	2.05
1.0 0.1	0.1	1.03	1.08	1.24	1.28
	0.2	1.07	1.17	1.32	1.42
	0.3	1.10	1.27	1.41	1.57
0.2	0.1	1.03	1.08	1.32	1.37
	0.2	1.06	1.16	1.39	1.50
	0.3	1.10	1.27	1.48	1.66
0.3	0.1	1.03	1.07	1.36	1.40
	0.2	1.06	1.16	1.42	1.53
	0.3	1.09	1.26	1.50	1.69

a/ P = proof load.

b/ $\bar{R}$ = mean target strength in design of structure.

3. Load factors for some typical applications

For the loads considered in AS 1170 [1], [2], the following are the statistical parameters stated in terms of the reliability theory used for the derivation of tables 15-18.

Design dead load, $S^* = L_D$: $V_S = 0.1$, $S^* = \bar{S}$, $S_{0.9} = 1.1 S^*$ (5)

Design wind gust load, $S^* = L_W$: $V_S = 0.2$, $S^* = S_{0.7}$, $S_{0.9} = 1.1 S^*$ (6)

Design floor live load, $S^* = L_L$: $V_S = 0.3$, $S^* = S_{0.9}$, $S_{0.9} = S^*$ (7)

where S^*, $\bar{S}$, $S_{0.7}$ and $S_{0.9}$ are the Code-specified design load, the mean, and the 70-percentile and 90-percentile values, respectively, of the probable peak load during the design lifetime of a structure. The statistical parameters used for the wind loads and live loads are based on data by Whittingham [13], and McGuire and Cornell [14], respectively.

The load factors given in equations (2) and (4) in the main text are derived from the use of equations (5) to (7) in this annex and the load factors in tables 16-18 with the parameter values $\alpha = 0.75$ and $C_{FSO} = C_{FS}/C_{FP} = 300$. These are typical parameters for structural units for which the consequences of collapse are great compared to the cost of the unit.

Table 18. Load factors for prototype testing

α	V_R	V_S	Load factor $K_U = R_{0.05}/S_{0.90}$				
			$C_{FSO} = 10$	$C_{FSO} = 30$	$C_{FSO} = 100$	$C_{FSO} = 300$	$C_{FSO} = 1,000$
0.5	0.1	0.1	1.15	1.26	1.39	1.52	1.68
		0.2	1.14	1.24	1.37	1.50	1.66
		0.3	1.17	1.28	1.42	1.55	1.71
	0.2	0.1	1.24	1.50	1.85	2.24	2.75
		0.2	1.18	1.42	1.75	2.12	2.61
		0.3	1.15	1.39	1.71	2.07	2.54
	0.3	0.1	1.30	1.75	2.42	3.25	4.49
		0.2	1.21	1.62	2.24	3.01	4.17
		0.3	1.15	1.54	2.13	2.86	3.96
0.75	0.1	0.1	1.11	1.22	1.34	1.47	1.62
		0.2	1.10	1.20	1.33	1.45	1.61
		0.3	1.13	1.24	1.37	1.50	1.66
	0.2	0.1	1.16	1.40	1.72	2.08	2.57
		0.2	1.10	1.33	1.63	1.97	2.43
		0.3	1.07	1.30	1.59	1.93	2.37
	0.3	0.1	1.17	1.57	2.17	2.91	4.03
		0.2	1.08	1.45	2.01	2.70	3.74
		0.3	1.03	1.38	1.91	2.57	3.55
1.0	0.1	0.1	1.09	1.19	1.31	1.45	1.59
		0.2	1.07	1.18	1.30	1.42	1.57
		0.3	1.11	1.21	1.34	1.47	1.62
	0.2	0.1	1.10	1.33	1.64	1.98	2.44
		0.2	1.05	1.26	1.55	1.88	2.31
		0.3	1.02	1.23	1.52	1.83	2.26
	0.3	0.1	1.08	1.45	2.00	2.69	3.73
		0.2	1.00	1.35	1.86	2.50	3.46
		0.3	0.95	1.28	1.77	2.37	3.28

4. Load factor for rare load events

The cost function C to be optimized for the derivation of a load factor has the general form

$$C = C_S + C_{FP} + p\xi p_F C_{FS} \qquad (8)$$

where C_S is the cost of the structure, C_{FP} and C_{FS} are the costs incurred if failure occurs during proof loading or in service, $p\xi$ is the probability that the rare load occurs and p_F is the probability of failure should the rare load occur.

It is apparent from the form of equation (8) that the load factor may be derived by assuming that the rare load does occur and that the cost incurred if failure occurs is $p\xi C_{FS}$.

B. Load factors for serviceability limit states

1. Method

A simple reliability model for the derivation of load factors for design to resist serviceability limit states has been described in a paper by Leicester and Beresford [15]. The model is presented in terms of two random variables, as illustrated in figure 64; these are the in-service value, denoted by Δ, and the complaint threshold value, denoted by Ω, of a serviceability parameter. Typical examples of the serviceability parameter are deflection and crack width. The input parameters for the model include the coefficients of variation V_Δ and V_Ω, the relative cost incurred if failure occurs, denoted by C_{FSO}, and a structural cost β that is defined in a manner analogous to α.

Figure 64. Distribution of serviceability parameter

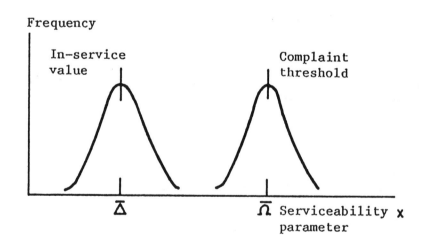

An example of the use of the model is given in figure 65, which shows design load factors computed for deflections, with the assumption that   and have Weibull distributions [5]. The load factor $\bar{\Omega}/\bar{\Delta}$ is not very sensitive to V_E, the uncertainty of stiffness, because of the large uncertainties of the in-service loads and complaint thresholds that must also be considered. This is a typical characteristic of load factors for serviceability limit states. Consequently, load factors to be used in load testing may be taken to be essentially similar to those used for design.

Figure 65. Load factors for design against excessive deflections

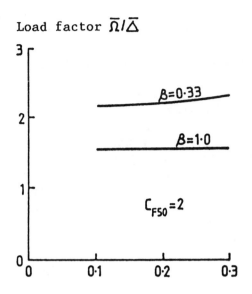

Coefficient of variation of stiffness V_E

2. Load factors for some typical applications

The load factors suggested in equations (3) and (5) of the main text represent an estimate based on the computed factors for several reliability models, such as that described in figure 65, together with a consideration of the statistical characteristics of real loads. Among these characteristics are the facts that the 10-year-return wind gust load is 0.6-0.7 times the magnitude of the 50-year-return wind [2] and that the arbitrary point-in-time value of a floor live load is on average only about 0.35 times the specified design live load and exceeds 0.7 times the specified design load for 10 per cent of the time [14].

Annex II

EXAMPLES OF CORRECTION FACTORS K_C FOR INCORRECT MODELLING
OF LOAD CHARACTERISTICS

A. Effects related to static characteristics

An example of this effect occurs when a timber beam that will be subjected in service to third-point loading is load-tested by a single central-point load. In this case, it is not sufficient to assess the performance of the beam solely in terms of the applied bending moment. The reason is that because the strength of a timber beam varies from point to point, there will be a greater probability of the peak bending moment occurring at a weak section in the case of a beam subjected to third-point loading than in the case of centre-point loading. This leads to an apparent decrease, typically of 20 per cent, in the nominal value of bending strength, and this must be covered by a corresponding adjustment of the K_C factor.

B. Effects related to stochastic characteristics

For many situations, the loads given in the SAA Loading Code [1], [2] are inadequate for use in load test specifications. This is because the deterministic format of the Code is too far removed from the characteristics of real loads. For example, many live loads such as crane and wind loads change rapidly with time and location in load histories that usually do not repeat. For these types of loads it is obviously not feasible to simulate all or even a small portion of all possible load histories, and consequently an idealized load or load sequence must be used in which the significant load parameters are correctly simulated. The correct parameter to be simulated in the specification of design loads depends on the response characteristics of the test structure. The following illustrates this point for the case of a load that fluctuates as a stationary Gaussian process and acts on a structure that has a design lifetime of T.

If the critical structural response is related to the peak load S_{max}, then the mean value $\bar{S}_{max}$ and coefficient of variation V_{smax} are given roughly by

$$\bar{S}_{max} = \sigma_S \sqrt{2 \ln(1.44 \, \nu T)}$$

$$V_{smax} = 1/\sqrt{2.4 \, \ln(\nu T)\ln(1.44 \, \nu T)}$$

in which

$$\sigma_S^2 = \int_0^\infty \phi(f) \, df$$

$$\nu^2 = \int_0^\infty f^2\phi(f) \, df / \int_0^\infty \phi(f) \, df$$

where $\phi(f)$ is the spectral density function of the load S.

If, on the other hand, the critical structural response is fatigue, then it is necessary that the specified loading programme correctly simulate load parameters that are related to fatigue. One important parameter for metal fatigue is h^4, where h is the peak-to-trough or trough-to-peak differential of a load change. For a narrow-band spectra, this mean differential is given by Yang [16]:

$$\Sigma h^4 = 128 \, \nu \, T\sigma_S^2$$

Other criteria for metal fatigue have been examined by Talreja [17] and Beck and Stevens [18].

Finally, the critical load parameter may relate to the duration of load. For the case of glass, this parameter is $\int_o^T S^{12}(t)\ dt$ [19] and may be evaluated from

$$\int_o^T S^{12}(t)\ dt = T\bar{S}^{12} \left\{ 1 + \sum_{N=2,4...}^{12} \left[\left(\frac{\sigma_S}{\bar{S}} \right)^N \frac{12}{\lfloor N \ \lfloor 12-N} \ 1,3,5,..(N-1) \right] \right\}$$

Apart from the choice of the correct load parameter to simulate, there are other difficulties with the specification of test loads that will not be discussed here. These include the choice of critical load combinations, such as the choice of peak load effect due to combined wind and crane live loads, and the choice of critical combined load effects, such as the combined racking and uplift forces that occur on shear walls of houses due to wind actions.

- 156 -

Annex III

EXAMPLES OF LOAD FACTORS FOR DURATION EFFECTS

Tables 19–21 give examples, taken from AS 1720–1975 [10], of the duration load factor K_D for use in load-testing timber structures for ultimate and serviceability limit states, respectively.

Table 19. Duration factor for load testing
timber structures to ultimate limit states:
duration load factor $K_{D'} = K_{D1}K_{D2}$

	K_{D1}	
Duration of load	Failure in timber	Failure of metal in metal connectors
5 seconds	0.9	1.0
5 minutes	1.0	1.0
5 days	1.3	1.0
5 months	1.5	1.0
5 years	1.6	1.0
50 years	1.8	1.0

	K_{D2}	
Structural component	Dry timber	Green timber
Tension members	1.0	1.0
Beams		
Slenderness coefficient $\leq$ 10	1.0	1.0
Slenderness coefficient $>$ 10	1.1	1.4
Columns	1.1	1.4
Metal connectors		
Failure in timber	1.0	1.2
Failure in metal	1.0	1.0

Table 20. Duration load factor for testing timber structures
to serviceability limit states: factor K_D for
deflections of solid timber

Duration of load [a]	Average initial moisture content	K_D	
		Bending, compression and shear K_2	Tension K_3
Long duration	> 25%	3	1.5
Long duration	< 15%	2	1
Short duration	Any	1	1

[a] Long duration loading refers to a load duration of
12 months or greater. Short duration loading refers to a
duration of 2 weeks or less. Creep factors for intermediate
durations of 2 weeks to 1 year and for initial moisture contents of 15-25 per cent may be obtained by linear interpolation.

Table 21. Duration load factor for testing timber
structures to serviceability limit states: factor
K_D for slip of mechanical fasteners

Duration of load	K_D			
	Nails		Bolts, split rings and shear plates	
	Unseasoned members	Seasoned members	Unseasoned members	Seasoned members
> 6 months	10	5	4	3
2 weeks– 6 months	3	2	2	2
5 min–2 weeks	1.5	1.5	1.5	1.5
< 5 min	1	1	1	1

Annex IV

EXAMPLE OF A QUALITY CONTROL CRITERION

The following is a simple example intended to indicate a method of incorporating into quality control criteria some of the considerations listed as important in section C.

For this example, it will be assumed that in the production of certain structural units it is found that a malfunction in the production process leads to a defect in a small proportion p_D of all the units produced thereafter until the malfunction is corrected. On average, the malfunction is found to occur once every m production units. If a structural unit with a defect is put into service, the probability of failure is p_F. The cost of undertaking a load test on a unit is C_T and the cost incurred if failure occurs in service is C_{FS}. The problem is to decide on the optimum frequency of sampling. This will be stated as one sample for every n structural units fabricated, where n is a large number.

The probability of encountering a defect for the first time on a given sample follows a geometric distribution and so, on average, the number of samples required to first encounter a defect is $1/p_D$.

Hence, the number of structural units put into service before the malfunction is detected is $(n-1)/p_D$ and the cost of failures is

$$(n - 1)p_F p_D C_F / p_D.$$

The total number of structural units fabricated between each malfunction is $m - (m/n)$, so the average cost of failure per structure in service is

$$(n - 1)p_F p_D C_F / p_D[m - (m/n)] \cong n p_F C_F / m.$$

The average cost of testing per structure in service is $C_T/(n-1) \cong C_T/n$.

Hence, the total cost per structure in service, denoted by C, is

$$C = C_T/n + n p_F C_F/m \qquad (14)$$

The optimum choice of the sampling interval n is given by $C/n = 0$, which leads to

$$n = \sqrt{C_T m / C_f p_F} \qquad (15)$$

For example, if $C_T = 5$, $C_F = 100$, $m = 10,000$ and $p_F = 0.05$, then the optimum sampling interval n is 100.

References

1. Standards Association of Australia, <u>Australian Standard 1170 Part 1-1971: SAA Loading Code Part 1 Dead and Live Loads</u> (Sydney, 1971).

2. Standards Association of Australia, <u>Australian Standard 1170 Part 2-1975: SAA Loading Code Part 2-Wind Forces</u> (Sydney, 1975).

3. R. Bares and N. Fitzsimons, "Load test of building structures", <u>American Society of Civil Engineers: Structural Division: Journal</u>, vol. 101, No. ST5, Proceedings Paper 11322 (May 1975), pp. 1111-1123.

4. Standards Association of Australia, <u>Australian Standard 1697-1975: SAA Gas Pipeline Code</u> (Sydney, 1975).

5. R. H. Leicester, "Proof grading, a practical application of reliability theory", <u>Proceedings of Third International Conference on Applications of Statistics and Probability in Soil and Structural Engineering</u>, vol. 1 (Sydney, Australia, January-February 1979), pp. 263-277.

6. J. B. Menzies, "Load testing of concrete building structures", <u>Structural Engineer</u>, vol. 56A, No. 12 (December 1978), pp. 347-353.

7. D. S. Jones and C. W. Oliver, "The practical aspects of load testing", <u>Structural Engineer</u>, vol. 56A, No. 12 (December 1978), pp. 353-356.

8. D. E. Allen, "Limit state design in Canada", <u>Building Research and Practice</u>, July/August 1976, pp. 226-231.

9. Standards Association of Australia, <u>Australian Standard 1649-1974: Determination of Basic Working Loads for Metal Fasteners for Timber</u> (Sydney, 1974).

10. Standards Association of Australia, <u>Australian Standard 1720-1975: SAA Timber Engineering Code</u> (Sydney, 1975).

11. R. H. Leicester, "Load factors for design codes", <u>Proceedings of Metal Structures Conference</u> (Adelaide, Australia, November 1976), pp. 94-98.

12. R. H. Leicester, "Load factors for design and testing", <u>Proceedings of 1977 Conference of Australian Fracture Group</u> (Melbourne, 25 October 1977).

13. H. E. Whittingham, "Extreme wind gusts in Australia", Bulletin No. 46 (Melbourne, Australia, Bureau of Meteorology, February 1964).

14. R. K. McGuire and C. A. Cornell, <u>American Society of Civil Engineers: Structural Division: Journal</u>, "Live load effects in office buildings", vol. 100, No. ST7, Proceedings Paper 10660 (July 1974), pp. 1351-1366.

15. R. H. Leicester and F. D. Beresford, "A probabilistic model for serviceability specifications", <u>Proceedings of Sixth Australasian Conference on the Mechanics of Structures and Materials</u> (Christchurch, New Zealand, University of Canterbury, August 1977), pp. 407-414.

16. J. Yang, "Statistics of random loading relevant to fatigue", <u>American Society of Civil Engineers: Structural Division: Journal</u>, vol. 100, No. EM3 (June 1974), pp. 469-476.

17. R. Talreja, "On fatigue life under stationary Gaussian loads", <u>Engineering Fracture Mechanics</u>, vol. 5, 1973, pp. 993-1007.

18. V. R. Beck and L. K. Stevens, "Wind loading failures of corrugated roof sheeting", <u>Proceedings of Diamond Jubilee Conference</u>, Even No. 310.2 (Perth, Australia, Institute of Engineers, April 1979), pp. 1-12.

19. D. E. Allen and W. A. Dagleish, "Dynamic wind loads and cladding design", <u>Proceedings of IABSE Conference on Repeated Loads</u> (Lisbon, International Association for Bridge and Structural Engineering, 1973).

Bibliography

Allen, D. E. Probabilistic study of reinforced concrete in bending. _Journal of the American Concrete Institute_ (Detroit, Michigan) 67:989-993, December 1970.

An investigation of the crack control characteristics of various types of bar in reinforced concrete beams. Research report 41,018. _By_ G. D. Base _and others_. London, Cement and Concrete Association, December 1966.

Ellingwood, B. R. _and_ A. H-S. Aug. Risk-based evaluation of design criteria. _American Society of Civil Engineers: Structural Division: Journal_ (New York) 100:ST9:1771-1788, September 1974. Proceedings paper 10778.

Jong-Chern, P. _and_ C. A. Cornell. Spatial and temporal variability of live loads. (New York) 99:ST5:903-922, May 1973. Proceedings paper 9747.

Paris, P. C. The fracture mechanics approach to fatigue. Fatigue - an interdisciplinary approach. _In_ Proceedings of 10th Sagamore Army Materials Research Conference. Syracuse, New York, 1964.

Pham, L. _and_ R. H. Leicester. Structural variability due to the design process. _In_ Proceedings of Third International Conference on applications of statistics and probability in soil and structural engineering, v.2. Sydney, Australia, January-February 1979. p. 586-600.

Walsh, P. F. Quality control of concrete by compressive strength testing. Report 15. Melbourne, CSIRO, Division of Building Research, 1973.

_____ Reinforced concrete deflection design. Report 39. Melbourne, CSIRO, Division of Building Research, 1975.

UNIDO GENERAL STUDIES SERIES

The following publications are available in this series:

Title	Symbol	Price (US$)
Planning and Programming the Introduction of CAD/CAM Systems A reference guide for developing countries	ID/SER.O/1	25.00
Value Analysis in the Furniture Industry	ID/SER.O/2	7.00
Production Management for Small- and Medium-Scale Furniture Manufacturers A manual for developing countries	ID/SER.O/3	10.00
Documentation and Information Systems for Furniture and Joinery Plants A manual for developing countries	ID/SER.O/4	20.00
Low-cost Prefabricated Wooden Houses A manual for developing countries	ID/SER.O/5	6.00
Timber Construction for Developing Countries Introduction to wood and timber engineering	ID/SER.O/6	20.00
Timber Construction for Developing Countries Structural timber and related products	ID/SER.O/7	25.00
Timber Construction for Developing Countries Durability and fire resistance	ID/SER.O/8	20.00
Timber Construction for Developing Countries Strength characteristics and design	ID/SER.O/9	25.00
Timber Construction for Developing Countries Applications and examples	ID/SER.O/10	20.00
Technical Criteria for the Selection of Woodworking Machines	ID/SER.O/11	25.00
Issues in the Commercialization of Biotechnology	ID/SER.O/13	45.00
Software Industry Current trends and implications for developing countries	ID/SER.O/14	25.00
Maintenance Management Manual With special reference to developing countries	ID/SER.O/15	35.00
Manual for Small Industrial Businesses Project design and appraisal	ID/SER.O/16	25.00

Forthcoming titles include:

Design and Manufacture of Bamboo and Rattan Furniture	ID/SER.O/12	

Please add US$ 2.50 per copy to cover postage and packing. Allow 4-6 weeks for delivery.

ORDER FORM

Please complete this form and return it to:

UNIDO Documents Unit (F-355)
Vienna International Centre
P.O. Box 300, A-1400 Vienna, Austria

Send me _____ copy/copies of _____

_____ (ID/SER.O/_____) at US$ _____ /copy plus postage.

PAYMENT

☐ I enclose a cheque, money order or UNESCO coupon (obtainable from UNESCO offices worldwide) made payable to "UNIDO".

☐ I have made payment through the following UNIDO bank account: CA-BV, No. 29-05115 (ref. RB-7310000), Schottengasse 6, A-1010 Vienna, Austria.

Name _____

Address _____

Telephone _____ Telex _____ Cable _____ Fax _____

Note: Publications in this series may also be obtained from:

Sales Section
United Nations
Room DC2-0853
New York, N.Y. 10017, U.S.A.
Tel.: (212) 963-8302

Sales Unit
United Nations
Palais des Nations
CH-1211 Geneva 10, Switzerland
Tel.: (22) 34-60-11, ext. Bookshop

✂

ORDER FORM

Please complete this form and return it to:

UNIDO Documents Unit (F-355)
Vienna International Centre
P.O. Box 300, A-1400 Vienna, Austria

Send me _____ copy/copies of _____

_____ (ID/SER.O/_____) at US$ _____ /copy plus postage.

PAYMENT

☐ I enclose a cheque, money order or UNESCO coupon (obtainable from UNESCO offices worldwide) made payable to "UNIDO".

☐ I have made payment through the following UNIDO bank account: CA-BV, No. 29-05115 (ref. RB-7310000), Schottengasse 6, A-1010 Vienna, Austria.

Name _____

Address _____

Telephone _____ Telex _____ Cable _____ Fax _____

Note: Publications in this series may also be obtained from:

Sales Section
United Nations
Room DC2-0853
New York, N.Y. 10017, U.S.A.
Tel.: (212) 963-8302

Sales Unit
United Nations
Palais des Nations
CH-1211 Geneva 10, Switzerland
Tel.: (22) 34-60-11, ext. Bookshop